You don't think as smart as you are.

What if Gerber got it wrong . . . and if Covey
was holding back . . .?

From where you are . . . to where you want to be
IN BUSINESS™

John Vamos
Karen McCreadie

IMPORTANT NOTE FROM THE AUTHOR

This note is not important because I wrote it, though that does count some, right? It is important because it will help put some of what lies ahead into context.

First, thank you for investing in this book.

This was my first publication and appeared in 2002 after a gestation period of close to a decade. In that time, I was singularly focused on explaining, in terms that reflected our neurology rather than our 'rah-rah', why we underperform. Why there is a gap between our performance at work and our **known-to-self** *potential.*

You Don't Think As Smart As You Are *is faithfully represented here in its* **original** *format,* **original** *text.*

Now, ordinarily you might learn a thing or two in the twenty years after publishing your first book. Authors reflect this by identifying 'editions' of their work. Well, I am pleased to say I have learnt a thing or two since this book first appeared. To that end, the two books I have published since 2002 reflect those learnings.

Between 2020 and 2010 my discoveries and thoughts were reflected in the second book and focused on the same dilemma, however specifically as it applies to workgroups.

Since 2010 my attention has been drawn to the application of these learnings in an effort to understand why, in many (or most) cases the more we succeed commercially, the more we fail personally.

Elephants and the Business Laws of Nature *(Book 2) was published in 2010,* **Four Voices** *(Book 3) in 2022.*

You will see references in this book to entities that have morphed since that time. Importantly, Business **Thinking** *Systems has become Business* **Coaching** *Systems and the army of coaches I once worked shoulder to shoulder with, and referenced in these pages, have each chartered their own course.*

You can now find me at www.bcscoach.com.au, the home of all things Thinking Systems and Business Coaching related.

I am also contactable at www.fourvoicesadvisory.com.au for those that seek to explore the work reflected in that third and most recent publication.

I hope you enjoy this book. I am proud to say that until there is an evolutionary 'revolution' in the design of our brains, it still rings true.

John Vamos
September 2022

Book production and text design by Publish Central
Cover design by Pipeline Design

Disclaimer

CONTENTS

FOREWORD

By Professor Stewart Clegg

I am a sociologist. That's my discipline. I am also a Business School professor in a School of Management. That's my job. Many times I have wondered why so much management theory is bad sociology (because it fails to connect with what people actually do when they do management) and why so few sociologists seem interested in what it is that managers ordinarily do. When they do get interested they often seem to do it for all the wrong reasons to apply some or other grand theory, some prescriptive viewpoint, to what people do.

There is one brand of sociology I have always had a soft spot for, more than any other, that has always eschewed grand theory, and that is one known as ethnomethodology. Horrible name, isn't it? But it is quite descriptive. It means, literally, 'folk methods' the methods that people ordinarily use to make sense in their everyday lives. It's progenitor, Harold Garfinkel, was deeply immersed in studying what he saw as the methods of everyday life the myriad ordinary ways in which, through which, by which, people make sense of each other and their doings.

John Vamos may have read Garfinkel at some time or had a class in ethnomethodology. I don't know, or he may have stumbled on some of the same insights for himself. It doesn't matter. He shares the same profound insight: that there is no need to step outside of everyday knowledge to tell people how to do what they do otherwise they wouldn't be able to do it. Sometimes, however, one needs to be able to bring how it is that people are able to do what they do to their attention, consciously, so that they can do it better.

People always know a lot more than they can say and they always have great depths of knowledge about what they do. And sometimes they don't know what it is that they do know: their knowledge is too tacit, too taken-for-granted, such that they are unable to easily explicate the grounds that make possible all that they do and all that they *could* do. The gap between what they do and what they could do is not one that is best plugged by what they don't know and that someone else – a management consultant, guru, or a lecturer – does know. It is plugged by making explicit all that they do know and draw on in doing what they usually do. Nobody knows their business better than they do. This is the fundamental insight of this book.

What the book provides is a way of unlocking all the taken-for-granted and tacit knowledge, the constitutive grounds that we all already have but either don't recognize or know about, yet implicitly trade off in our everyday business life. This book will help you unlock those Thinking Systems through techniques that anyone can learn and apply and profit from.

Think of this book as an 'ethnomethodology' for everyday business life. Apply it to your business life. And profit from what you already know but did not know you knew which this book will help you discover.

Stewart Clegg
School of Management
University of Technology, Sydney

ON ACKNOWLEDGEMENTS

This book was made possible by the commitment and support of my co-author Karen McCreadie and a few bottles of red wine of mixed quality.

Karen's ability to hear what I'm saying, yet know what I meant, is uncanny. Her sense of humour, positive attitude and commitment to her craft are inspiring and I look forward to her contribution to the next book.

There are a number of people responsible for this book, and the thinking behind it. I will save my thanks to them for the end, because if this thinking has the profound and positive effect on you as it has on me, then you should find out who they are after you read the book. That way the acknowledgements may have the impact they deserve.

ABOUT BUSINESS THINKING SYSTEMS (WWW.BUSINESSTHINKING.COM.AU)

Business Thinking Systems (BTS) is an international consultancy delivering strategic, operational and personal performance improvement programs across a wide variety of industries and sizes of business.

The company was formed in 1995 by the author to deliver a unique business process model and now has a network of active business coaches in Australia, New Zealand and Singapore.

By implementing the Thinking System tools described in this book, BTS coaches have reached over 3,000 workgroups in more than 2,000 enterprises of all sizes in 4 countries.

The Statistics quoted in these pages are distilled from a database that has tracked this activity over the last six years. *They represent verifiable outcomes generated by BTS business coaches during this period.*

TERMINOLOGY

Before we start on our journey we need to explain one thing about terminology:

This book is designed for Business Owners, Managers, Team Leaders, Work-group Leaders, and Department Heads – basically anyone whose job it is to manage people. Rather than repeat this list throughout the book, I will use one of the terms with the intention to describe all these stakeholders.

Part One:

THE JOURNEY

'Don't start a marathon with a hole in your sandshoe'

People do business with people they like. Typically people like people who think similarly. If I like the way you think, chances are I will like the way you deal with the problems we face. This allows us to get quickly to the point of deciding whether there is a basis for a business relationship or not.

Part one of this book is intended to serve the same purpose. I want you to find out early if you have a degree of empathy for the thinking and attitude that inspired the science behind the Thinking System. To do this I have outlined some of the observations, experiences and points of view that are important to me. If they strike a chord for you then I am sure the conclusions that follow will be powerful tools for you, in both your business and personal life.

1

WHAT'S THE *REAL* PROBLEM . . .

I've had a number of false starts with this book, Of the three types of 'writer's block' ('what to write?', 'how to write it?' and 'why to write it?') I am so very fortunate to have suffered from the third and I will explain why shortly.

We are well into 'the information age'. We live in a world where there is no shortage of problems (including business productivity problems). We have literally hundreds of thousands of business consultants who have made it their life work to name and describe the various types of business productivity problems and then set out to provide solutions for them.

It is an industry that 'feeds on itself' and in this respect is not unlike the virus industry in computing. A hacker devises and releases a virus. The virus eradication industry gives it a name (if it does not already have one) and devotes enormous resources to neutralizing it and releasing 'a fix'. When this is achieved the process repeats itself. What sustains the virus eradication industry is that new viruses are being released on a regular basis so that there is a constant need for software 'upgrades'.

Virus software provides a 'temporary fix' until the next virus comes along. There are no apparent attempts to eradicate software vandalism at source. The problem has been defined as 'our current software does not address virus X' whereas the underlying problem actually is that software terrorism exists on a wide and increasing scale.

The 'business solutions' industry is similar. Billions of dollars are generated in the process of naming, describing and providing so called 'solutions' to business productivity problems and yet 'the pain persists'. Virus software at least provides some temporary protection whereas the much-anticipated benefits of the various business solutions on offer generally remain illusory.

Now coming back to my 'writer's block' when I started writing this book I was sharing the industry wide illusion that 'business solutions fix business problems'.

I was driven to offer many good business solutions, based on a lot of practical experience, yet when I put them on paper they somehow seemed to become part, once again of the problem rather than the solution.

It took me a while to realise that there was no need to add more business solutions precisely because there was nothing wrong with the solutions already on offer in the first place. What was wrong was that these solutions simply addressed symptoms of an underlying problem. What was missing, until now was a clear, definitive understanding of that underlying problem which simply manifested in a variety of recognised business challenges.

My quest began whilst sitting in one of the many seminars and conferences I attended.

While we waited in hushed expectation for the words of a world renowned speaker I reflected on the extravagant claims of the promotional materials and the high expectations of those who had parted with hundreds of dollars to be there.

At an emotional level, as participants we were looking for and expecting answers to a long list of problems that had been identified on the glossy flyers. At first I thought that it was the cynic in me that doubted that the claims would be substantiated and lives would indeed be changed. Then I realised it was just the realist in me.

I started to perceive the enormous human wastage. As a result of this 'gathering of the perennially hopeful' the convenors would make money; the speakers would make money; the venue would make money; but the audience was unlikely to get it's money's worth in terms of medium to long term results.

WHY?

Because the conversion of an idea into action rarely takes place. This is true for all of us to a greater or lesser extent.

On the 'conversion scale' of being able to translate what I was hearing into what I was doing, I felt I was better than most. At first I was tempted to think that the 'others' were not as smart, not as dedicated and or not as committed to their craft as I was.

Clearly this was pure arrogance. By any objective measure there were many people in the room who were just as committed to obtaining a result as I was and others who were smarter and more capable.

It was then that I started to realize that the problem was not one of motivation, ability, sincerity or even personal honesty. The issue was that our ability to take what we hear and turn it into actions, protocols and procedures is *inherently* limited.

BUT WHY?

What is it that makes it so hard for us to convert ideas into action, for us to be the living expression of what we know, what we've heard and what we think is best?

Clearly conferences are not very effective. However the industry continues to thrive based on a set of generally accepted myths.

This conversion problem is the basis of the Conference Industry's *Myth Number One,* it goes something like this: 'If you can get just one good idea out of this presentation/workshop/speech/weekend, it will have been worth the time and cost that you have expended.'

Maybe; maybe not. My suspicion is that this is something like a virus fix. They are at best presenting a temporary solution that will necessitate your return to the seminar theatre for the 'refresher course'.

Conference *Myth Number Two*: states that 'It's our job (say the speakers) to share the information; whether you use it or not is your problem'. This is an amazing argument to hear from 'change specialists.' Surely the quality of the message should be judged not by the content alone or even by the convertibility of the content into action; it should be judged by what actually happens as a result of the investment.

Myth Number Three is the myth of complicity. It's like this. Our general shortcomings as humans in our business and personal endeavors, has created a large market for more and more 'solutions'. In other words, we don't convert existing ideas into action but demand new ones instead. So all these speakers (from the gifted business guru's like those acknowledged in the sub-title of this book, to the snake oil salesman travelling the world selling new solutions – *their* versions of other peoples ideas) all keep churning out new 'ways' to look at the same old problems. And incidentally new ways to make a living!

In its consistent failure to deliver sustained, promised change, the business solutions industry has clearly conned its customers.

Its customers, on their part, have colluded with the industry by failing to challenge the three myths. (Can it be that many have been sponsored by employers to attend and are unwilling to report that results were nil or negligible for fear that their next application to attend a seminar will be refused?)

Whatever the reason The essential question business educators face is not 'What's missing from our solutions tool-kit?' The question is "what's wrong with the conversion rate" or better yet, as we will discover in the pages to come, what's wrong with *us*? And the answer is 'Just about everything'.

I realised that the *problem is not the content it is the context. The challenge is not in perfecting the information; it is instead perfecting the translation or conversion of the idea.* It is the lack of any attempts to even begin to tackle that challenge that *haunts us and holds us back.*

The real need therefore is to find ways to support people to turn ideas into actions. We need to support people with achievable, bulletproof protocols, so that they can become the living expression of *any* appropriate or chosen way.

Gerber and the theorists did get it wrong when they typically offered the panacea and said 'You know you *should* spend 10% of your time on the business, applying the principles in his book.' The principles are great and powerful and worthy of their popularity, but I know for a fact that students of the material are no better a reflection of the potential that lies in the application of those principles than those who are ignorant of them.

Covey's *seven habits of highly effective people* are not habits at all. They are coincidences, characteristics that you happen to find in successful people.

What if I said re Gerber that it is 'impossible, biologically, for anyone to work on their business and not in it'.

And what if I said re Covey that (surprise-surprise) you can't change people – so you have to work with the 'habits' you already have?

Given this, can we still improve our lives and business performance? You bet we can!

My journey's end was the realisation that the problem is this: *if we are to convert ideas towards improved or perfect business performance we face a deep-seated biological challenge, not a superficial one.*

All the business books I've read are about from the 'tip of your nose' forward, yet the real challenge is in the opposite direction, from the tip of your nose backwards into the core, biological realities of how we think.

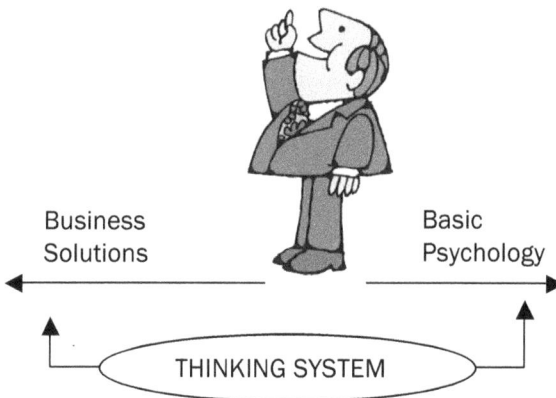

Business Solutions ← → Basic Psychology

THINKING SYSTEM

Figure 1: Context of business books

Even more fortunate for me, as I indicated, I found the solutions I was offering before I fully understood this challenge. I found them by inadvertently taking on the responsibility for making up the gap between performance and potential for my clients. I was then able to work out what was *missing* from their thinking, and fill in the blanks. I then realised that there was a *formula* for filling in those blanks and so, hopefully, from the pages ahead, you will get both, in less than the ten years it took me to be able to offer them.

2

THE TWO KNOWLEDGE GAPS

There are two 'knowledge gaps'. The first is the gap between what you *know* and what you *apply*.

The second is the gap between what you *know* and what you *don't know*.

In the first, what's missing is simply the translation of ideas into action or the know-how. Sounds right and logical . . . but *wrong*! A simple and compelling conclusion but *wrong*. After a decade pulling apart and putting together businesses it is clearly evident to me that when you have the 'know' you most often *have* the 'know-how'. So what *really* makes this 'translation' (of idea into action) a challenge is the question.

Note also that this 'first gap' is the part of the performance equation that Coaching addresses.

The obvious question is 'why don't we use the knowledge we have?' This book answers that question.

In the second gap, the missing ingredient *is* the knowledge. With respect to this gap, we might well ask 'Why do we search for new knowledge when the first "gap" is still evident and holding us back?'. Or ask 'Is it not more appropriate to use what we have before we add more "stock"?'

Quite probably. That is, if we actually applied what we already knew, we would probably discover the information or knowledge we feel is lacking as part of the very application process and so would not need to seek new knowledge or work on the second gap instead of the first.

> **'If we all used all that we knew, we would be a lot less concerned about what we don't know'**

The *Performance* problem obviously lies in the first gap – between what we know and what we apply. If we all used all that we knew, we would be a lot less concerned about what we don't know.

The crazy thing is that people try to solve the first gap (performance) by working on the second gap (knowledge). The presumption is that the first gap is *due* to the second! In other words, if a business or an individual is not performing to their best, if they are not the living expression of the best they can be, they respond by seeking more/new knowledge.

We do this by training our staff, attending more courses and, dare I say it, hiring consultants. All of which ends up adding to the 'what', without in any way resolving the 'how'.

Now I am not suggesting that we stop seeking new information, knowledge and ideas. Field experience has proven time and again that *potential improves as you journey <u>towards</u>* it. The more I work on converting my potential into performance the more my potential expands.

So what am I trying to say? Stop trying to learn new stuff and use the concepts in this book to unlock your ability to use what you already have. Then let the journey that propels you towards your potential, help identify what it is you *don't* know, that you really *should* know!

3

YOU DON'T THINK AS SMART AS YOU ARE

So . . . what do <u>you</u> think?

The conference or seminar scene is pretty much always the same; the audience waits for the speaker with anticipation, digesting the smorgasbord of hyperbole that constitutes the usual MC's introduction. Already the message is under pressure to live up to their expectations.

For me, as the speaker, the opening is pretty much standard. I begin by asking the audience:

'Who already uses every good idea they have ever heard? Whose business and lifestyle is supported by bullet proof protocols that have ensured that each day is an expression of the best that they already know or could be?'

The answer is always the same – nobody.

The next question is therefore obvious . . .

'So, what the hell are you *doing* here?'

I mean, why reach out for new ideas when you are not yet utilising fully the ideas you already have? This universal acceptance that it's OK to be a fraction of your potential is annoying. It is this gap that has fascinated and continues to fascinate me. My pursuit of the answer led to this book and, before, to the emergence of the first real Coaching Discipline in the world outside sport . . . the Thinking System.

There is another part to this question.

I then ask the audience: "Who's in charge of what we think?"

> **You are <u>so</u> not in control of your thinking that it's not funny, it's scary!**

And again the answer is pretty much standard – 'we are' is the chorus.

Then I ask them . . . 'Who is going to win the next Grand Final or the next election, or which religion makes most sense?'

What follows is a great debate as they engage each other with their various points of view. Sometimes, if I am really lucky, they might even fight amongst themselves! Then I ask them whether on their way to this productivity forum or coaching workshop, whatever it is we happen to be conducting, they intended or expected to be spending what I usually allow to be 5–10 minutes, debating politics, religion and sport? The answer of course is 'No'.

So I ask . . . 'then *why* did you?' They respond as one . . . 'because *you* asked us the question'.

My indignant and usually animated response to that is . . . 'Don't you dare try to pull that stunt on me! I just asked you who's in charge of what you think and you said *you were*! And now *you* want to blame *me* for wasting the last ten minutes!'

At this point the penny drops for some:

You are <u>so</u> not in control of your thinking that it's not funny, it's scary!

Your thoughts are reactions to what you see, what you hear and much more. The car that pulls out of the intersection and in front of you without indicating, could steal your thoughts for an hour. Your family, your staff, your colleagues are all much more in charge of what you think about than you will ever be!

At best, at 10pm, in front of an open fire, with a cognac in one hand and a cigar in the other . . . and it has been 2 solid hours since you last spoke to anyone . . . then for a minute you might be in charge. Or first thing in the morning (for a few minutes) you may be in control of what you think. The rest of the time you simply *are not*.

This single phenomenon is the most significant reason we perform at a level that is well below our potential. It is not attitude, commitment, resources, or knowledge or *anything* that holds us up in the pursuit of our potential more than this one fact.

You do not think as smart as you are, because you are not in charge of what you think! This book is totally dedicated to turning this tide around in your favour by helping you understand this, and the related thinking challenges we all face. And it's also about providing you with the tool kit to let you take charge.

LET'S GO BACK TO MY AUDIENCE

Someone in the audience usually protests once I have dismissed them for daring to suggest that the debate about the relative merits of Taoism was my fault. "I didn't go along with you (someone will inevitably plead) . . . I, instead, was thinking 'why is he asking all these dumb and irrelevant questions?'"

Fact is, it doesn't matter. Whatever the thinking happened to be it was triggered by *me*, the speaker, not by the audience member's dissenting thoughts. It was all around one thing . . . *my* questions. The audience members were all thinking something that was in every sense triggered by me.

> **We might be in charge of our opinion (although even that is debatable) but we are definitely not in charge of our thinking.**

We might be in charge of our opinion (although even that is debatable) but we are definitely not in charge of our thinking.

There is an upside and a downside to becoming aware of this. The downside is obvious . . . you realise you are a walking reaction . . . The upside? It is *huge.* You see, if people are not in charge of their thinking, and you know why and how this 'phenomena' works, then you can put yourself in charge of what the people around *you* are thinking – and that is powerful stuff!

13

4

YOUR PERFORMANCE GAP

So if we have established that you are not using all the good ideas you have ever had and if it's your business and/or your responsibility to improve things, how likely do you think it is that your employees or colleagues are using all their good ideas?

HIGHLY UNLIKELY!

(By the way, if you don't employ people, but rely on others to do their job *well*, before you can do yours perfectly, you are in the same situation.)

> **Closing the gap between performance and potential is the domain of coaching; changing potential is the domain of teaching and consulting. This book is about coaching!**

Now, you may be thinking to yourself that all reading this book is going to do is to give you more ideas that you can feel guilty about not implementing! Well, I promise that it *will* give you new ideas but they will be given to you as a *means* to *immediately* reduce the performance gap. And, hopefully in a way that will inspire you and excite you to embrace and apply them. The intent of this book is to bridge the gap between information and implementation – I don't want to change you . . . I just want to make it easy for you to reduce the performance gap, OK?

Closing the gap between performance and potential is the domain of coaching; changing potential is the domain of teaching and consulting. This is about coaching!

14

It's about _why_ this happens and it's not about trying to extend what you could be to what someone else thinks you ought to be. I intend to give you a better understanding of the challenges you face. More often than not we know what we should be doing but for some reason we don't seem to do it. I will explain the inescapable biological reasons for this and provide you with solutions too. Giving you an insight into the characteristics or behaviour that you simply need to mimic to get more of the desired results.

My biggest bugbear in management and business today is that there is a plethora of books (and gurus) preaching 'their' ideas. But the fact that it worked for them does not mean it will work for you, even if it is a valid solution. Just because it sounds like it works doesn't mean you can make it yours. Just because every part of you relates to the 'idea' that doesn't mean you can translate it into reality. This book, on the other hand, allows you to find out how to make your thinking more effective so that you can define and refine _your own way_.

Not everything here, like any other book I guess, is a first. The original theories behind any of today's popular practices are simply studies of human behaviour, just like this. There's no such thing as a 'management' guru. There never has been and there never will be. There are however people who from a commercial perspective, observe human behaviour and report on it. They are simply correspondents.

Think about it . . . It's like crediting the war correspondent with the victory of the battle. Yet all she did was be there and tell the world what she saw.

In contrast, I have been a practitioner, and this is about my experience with or of human behaviour and how I have seen it both assist and destroy companies. All I want is for you to be able to harness your thinking, and the thinking of those around you, to build your business and create an environment that people feel valued and happy in.

5

THE MIRACLE OF BUSINESS

Jane is a Real Estate Agent; she went to Tech and completed all the qualifications she needs to open her own Real Estate Agency. Simon is an Architect; he went to University to become a designer of homes or outdoor spaces. You would agree that what Jane does, day by day, is very different to what Simon does. Not only is what they do different, but the environment in which they do it and the tools they use are all very different.

But something miraculous happens when one day Jane, the Real Estate Agent opens a Real Estate Agency and Simon the Architect opens a practice. On that day they go from having two completely different jobs to having exactly the same job.

For both of them *from this point forward* it's about getting the most out of their people. Do *that* job well, and if those people happen to be selling homes, they'll sell many. If they happen to be designing homes, they'll design them well. But Jane's and Simon's jobs are now the same.

And, note it's a biological challenge they face not a commercial one.

The biggest mistake we can make is to draw a connection between commerce and people management as though the two were synonymous. One is cause the other is effect. They are not

> **But something miraculous happens when one day Jane, the Real Estate Agent opens a Real Estate Agency and Simon the Architect opens a practice.**
>
> **One that day they go from having two completely different jobs to having exactly the same job.**

16

the same. There is nothing *Business* about people management, and people management is the *one job* that every business owner on the planet has in common (more about this later).

The irony of this 'reality' is that people management is not covered in the Tech course on Real Estate. Nor is it covered in the syllabus for the Degree in Architecture. Yet the moment Jane and Simon go into business they are expected to be experts in it.

And people-management – sorry . . . *thinking*-management is what this is all about. If you are a workgroup leader or if you expect to have influence on those around you then your job is to step up and accept the challenge. In my experience very few people realise or understand the challenge, let alone accept it. This book is about the behaviour that will allow you to own and even enjoy that job. You don't have to know the theory behind the practical ideas just practice the behaviour and enjoy the results!

But knowing that this 'Miracle' is the true challenge of business is just the start of the problem. Consider this . . .

Jane and Simon were never taught many other necessary business skills such as finance, marketing, advertising, business building and relationship management. There are six near-universal business core functions:

1. Planning,
2. Finance,
3. Operations,
4. Sales & Marketing,
5. Human Resources and
6. Technology.

Add to these the specific tasks arising from whatever the business does. In business each of those 'common functions' listed above are disciplines that have tertiary qualification(s) attached to them. Some people dedicate their *lives* to being good at *just one*!

Now Jane may be the best Salesperson the world has ever seen but the moment she starts 'Jane's Real Estate' she's expected to have 6 degree's! No wonder the small business failure rate is so enormous!

The fundamental issue we have to contend with is this:

The *very things* that made Jane and Simon want to be a Real Estate Agent or Architect will probably *preclude* them from having the personal characteristics needed to be good at the other core functions. The detail driven, logic and left brain thinking of the finance person is for example very different from the right brain, creative marketing person.

(And even if it were possible for Jane to limit her work-on-the-business to the recommended 10%, the remaining 90% of her capacity would not be enough to enable her to substitute for the missing degrees, or different personality style.)

But suddenly these other core functions have risen to the top of the priority list whether they recognise it or not.

If this is the miracle of business, and it is, then business success is itself a miracle. Think about the average small to medium enterprise. To make it work you employ people with a range of skill sets. These skills are typically found in people of different background, knowledge and experience. It can even be said that different jobs can draw people from different socioeconomic backgrounds as well! They come together in business with a package of 'goods' from personality to qualifications that are inherently different from each other. *And,* they remind each other of these differences in almost every interaction they have.

Look at the above list of business core functions. I know some people who have dedicated their lives to Human Resource Management, they have at least one, sometimes more degrees to prove it . . . *and they are still ordinary at it!* (I hope they aren't reading this book!)

But for Jane and Simon, it becomes their primary responsibility the day they go into business or accept responsibility for a team.

But it's OK because all you need to do is *buy a popular business book and spend time on your business* and hey presto!

Sorry, the book might be written in English, but to Jane and Simon it's *Double Dutch*. And if this wasn't true then the bookshelf behind the business owner would have a profound effect on the business instead of gathering dust and looking impressive!

We know that there is a gap between performance and potential. Nobody disputes that. What is also evident is that the core cause of the problem seems to be elusive! I say this because if the traditionally accepted reasons or explanations for the gap were determined, then at least *one* of the millions of business books published would have become known to hit on at least *one* universally applicable solution. That has unfortunately not been the case. There seems to be no one book that stands today offering an unqualified solution to the core cause of the performance gap.

Here we uncover both the cause – that is the *real* problem – and for the first time the essential techniques for closing that gap.

6

HOW BIG IS THE PROBLEM:
Two incentives to pay attention

So far we've talked concepts. Let's get down to specifics – some numbers. Let's see if we can quantify the problem. My reflections on the gaps between performance and potential and coaching and biology might make good coffee table discussion but in order to inspire you, we need to quantify the problem.

If we show what these limitations actually cost, it might help you get enough motivation to pay attention!

The figures and calculations below are a summary of outcomes from over a decade in the field, coaching businesses and coaching coaches. The sample covers every business type and industry involving over 20,000 people in business and 3000 workgroups. In all, the study took in excess of 50,000 hours *not* including the time of our clients and their staff.

INCENTIVE TO PAY ATTENTION NUMBER ONE – THE STAFF VALUE EQUATION

Let's say 100% is the capability of a staff member who is actually applying everything they know on the job. Or to put it another way, 100% represents an individual who has no new good ideas or unused potential left because he or she is applying all of it.

What score would you give yourself on a scale from 0% to 100%?

At the time of writing this book I will have asked this question of over 3000 business owners, and the answer I get back is somewhere between 55% and 65%. Occasionally somebody says 5%, and we immediately take them out the back for some prozac and crisis counselling! Typically the benchmark is between 55% and 65%.

So for the sake of this demonstration let's take the mid-point of 60%:

If you have ten staff members and you pay them, on average, $50,000 – that's a $500,000 wage bill every year. If you're getting 60% out of them, 60% of half a million is $300,000. Meaning that you are paying half a million dollars to get $300,000 worth of their potential. In this case the 'Staff Value Deficiency' is $200,000.

Wage Bill	$500,000
Percentage of Potential applied @ 60%	$300,000
Staff Value Deficiency	$200,000

Figure 2: The Arithmetic of Staff Value Deficiency

This 'Deficiency' of $200,000 will still pick you up a nice two bedroom home in the outer suburbs of many cities where this book is being read.

So most businesses this size are giving away a two bedroom home *every year* in the difference between what they're *paying for* and what they're *getting* from their staff.

But what happens to your *wage* bill if you close this gap?

Nothing.

If you can do things that drive the team to 80 or 90% performance expressed as a function of potential, your payroll does not move. OK, if you sustain this and turn up for work having traded in the Commodore for a Ferrari, then the team might tap you on the shoulder and talk pay increases with you. So in time there may be some wage pressures. But in the first instance there won't be. You close the performance gap and it costs you nothing.

Will you ever get 100%?

No, because people are people, not machines. But you should be able to get 80% or 90% and that can mean a huge difference to your profitability or productivity without spending an extra cent.

INCENTIVE TO PAY ATTENTION NUMBER TWO – SCARY FACTS

What happens when you unpack and rebuild over 3000 workgroups? That 'unpacking' means we dissect each business or workgroup and assess its performance on every single process. This four-part activity has lead to many amazing and 'scary' statistics. Now don't try this at home folks but these are the real facts.

First we ask, 'what are the major components of your job or your workgroup?' Any collection of 13 to 16 people will identify a 'top ten components'. Let's call these 10 components – Core Functions. If we then go on and ask the workgroup to break these Core Functions down into their key actions or tasks, they will ultimately determine that there are around 270–330 tasks that in total make up those Core Functions, tasks that when completed deliver the outcome for the workgroup.

So basically there are 300 different things that need to be done for a business or workgroup to deliver what it promises.

Curiously enough, with 13 to 16 people in the room this number rarely changes, whether you're a football club, a baker or a real estate business.

The second step is to go through each one of those 300 activities one by one and challenge the workgroup on their performance. How well they feel each is done?

One of the answers they're allowed to give is –

'This task is done as well as could be expected by this team'.

In other words they are allowed to say to the coach 'With the team we have and the resources at our disposal we do this as well as we can'.

Here's a thing for you to ponder . . . Imagine we are standing in front of a workgroup. They have listed the 300 odd tasks or procedures that make up their business. If we then asked them the above question in relation to *each and every one* of these 300 plus discrete activities, what percentage of them do you think our workgroup would identify as fitting the category of tasks *done as well as could be expected?*

> So basically there are 300 different things that need to be done for a business or workgroup to deliver what it promises.

The answer is always 15% – an outcome that surprises almost everyone.

That means 85% of the tasks this workgroup (any workgroup) performs have been identified as having 'potential to improve' (It is important that you appreciate that 'potential to improve' here means with the existing team and its resources). Stage three of the process is to go through and have them tell us how each of these processes *should* be done. Effectively, they are setting their own benchmarks.

And finally, stage four where the workgroup tells you what's possible. Question: How long do you think it would take the workgroup, having agreed performance could be improved, to set each individual benchmark for improvement?

Answer: In a flash! Why? Because they knew the answer, even before the coach arrived.

Just think about that for a moment . . .

The existing team already knows that 255 of all the tasks they do in the course of their day (which represent 85% of everything that happens in the business) can be improved. They also think they know how to improve them!

But can they *really*? Our experience with over 3000 workgroups confirms that the team is correct – about 80% of the time. In other words, of those 255 activities they *think* they can fix (with existing resources and personnel) they actually *can* fix 204 of them. The remaining 51 can then be solved with more intensive analysis.

So the paradox behind these 'scary facts' is this, your staff are not implementing new or existing ideas that could be saving or making you a great deal of money. Those same staff members already know how to make your business more profitable and efficient without sending them to another training course or conference, but they don't do it!

> There is a paradox behind these 'scary facts':
>
> Your staff are not implementing ideas that could be saving or making you a great deal of money right now!
>
> Yet those same staff members already know how to make your business more profitable and efficient – without having to go to another training course or conference . . .

23

And the answer to the Question 'Why don't they? is not the answer we've been asked to believe. The real answer is disclosed in Part II. Before we explore it though, let's stick with these 'scary facts' and their implications.

Now, whose problem is this? Whose job is it to close this 'gap'? Where does the buck stop to erase the 'Staff Value Deficiency' and to close the performance gap, to elevate the business to a reasonable percentage of things being done perfectly?

Quite likely, yours – the business owner's, workgroup leader's or department manager's.

Of course, we've already established that you've had all the requisite training in all the core areas . . . NOT!

So far then:

We accept that we don't use all our good ideas. We've looked at what that costs us in our business. We have reluctantly accepted that it's our job to fix it but we also recognize that we don't have the resources or qualifications to fix everything.

Can it be fixed?

MINING OUR 'THINKING' POTENTIAL

Yes it can. By finally learning to harness the power to think so we can find and implement our own solutions. I say finally because whatever it is that our thinking process allows us to do, which is quite miraculous, the reality is that there is a huge gap between what it can do and what it actually does. More importantly, what we think it *ought* to do for us, and what it *actually* can do on its own.

Our thinking is limited. It is a little like having a McLaren F1, the fastest road car on the planet, 0–100 in 3.2 seconds, top speed of 387kph and only using it to travel two blocks down the road to get the milk in the morning!

There are several fundamental challenges that cause our thinking to fall far short of our capacity and therefore cause the Performance Gap.

So let's look at the ideas, techniques and the practice – if you are willing to try them, which can transform your business. There will be a number of components to this.

Part one, which you are reading now will help you decide if you relate to the challenges in the same way as I do.

In Part Two we will unpack the limitations of our thinking. There are four key limitations that you need to be aware of; a chapter is dedicated to each one.

This investigation then leads us to a powerful set of techniques for minimising the impact of those limitations – The Thinking System – this is detailed in Part Three

Then finally in Part Four we will look at the applications of those Thinking Systems in a workgroup environment so that you can become a *shortcut* between your team's performance and its potential. Being practical you can't do it all for yourself, as part of the problem is you. In the same way that most people won't get fit without a companion or a fitness trainer. But we will help you make a start. The approach I have chosen is to explain to you the behaviours we find in workgroups where the limitations are being minimised, all-be-it unconsciously! There are 7 of these (the number has no significance!). Matched to each of these behaviors will be Thinking Systems that will help you drive them in your business.

Will you be able to use them? Well, if you are capable of asking *questions*, you can. And unless you have never asked a question before, you won't even have to change your 'habits'.

Woven into all sections of the book will be pointers to assist you in applying the Thinking System to your business with or without the help of an external business coach, or a trained facilitator.

SO WHAT'S THE DESTINATION?

One of the key practices within Business Thinking Systems is what we call Destinations. Contemplation of the destination is in effect reverse engineering the path (yes, I know it has been said before but what hasn't been said is how do you make it a reality if you are not a Rocket Scientist or closely related to Einstein). You do have to know where you are going in order to get there as quickly and efficiently as possible – that is not a breakthrough, folks, its just obvious. Applying that here means you need to know where you can confidently expect to get to by reading this book.

The Destination I propose is simply this:

Our performance gap is related to the biological limitations to our thinking. *Managing* peoples thinking can overcome these limitations. This makes up for the biological limitations by building external thinking links where the internal ones are missing. That *management* involves applying the tools we have defined as 'Thinking Systems'. Those Thinking Systems are not dependent on your *circumstances*; they are dependent on the *outcomes* you want to deliver. In business the outcomes are universal, not specific (ie profit, efficiency, positive culture). Therefore the Thinking System is by nature 'formulaic'. So you can gain a substantial appreciation of them in these pages.

WHAT ABOUT A PLUG FOR BUSINESS COACHING?

I will make no apologies for my belief in Business Coaching. *You don't think as smart as you are* is a shameless and passionate advocacy of Business Coaching for business owners and workgroup leaders. However this is not a book about selling the benefits of business coaching. It is a book that will allow you to add significant value to your business whether you choose to involve a coach in your business or not.

Of course I hope that you will choose to employ a coach simply because of the difference it can make to your thinking. But if you choose not to I will provide you with practical tools that you can implement yourself.

There will be a future, I promise you when the first thing people will do after they decide to go into business is choose a business coach.

Yesterdays accountant (most of whom are still practicing today!) will be replaced by tommorrow's Business Coach – now that coaches can have some science behind their methods.

But that future is not here yet and until it is I want you to be successful and enjoy the decision you made to go into business or to be a leader or a manager of people. I want you to capture or recapture that euphoria that you felt when you made that decision. I want you to finally have the freedom you felt you would get when you started your own business. I want you to work less for yourself than you did for other people. I want you to be happy with that decision, not curse it every morning as you head into another crisis and another drama. And most of all I want you to be successful – whatever that means for you . . .

7

RULES FOR THE ROAD

Ideas are everywhere. Everyone you meet has the newest, greatest idea to emerge onto the planet. The fact that a few thousand people have probably thought of it before is irrelevant.

But ideas are useless without action.

So I genuinely don't want you to buy this book unless you are going to take action.

People write books for a number of reasons – ego, necessity, love, passion – whatever it may be. People read books for a number of reasons too – for gathering information, for knowledge, for fun or just something to pass the time at the airport.

I want this book to make a difference to your business and therefore to your life. I want you to read it with the clear intention that you will implement whatever comes to you in the process – and I am confident you will be rewarded.

I have a theory that everybody's brain has an unused-new-idea-ometer. Because you don't use your good ideas, you forget them and eventually, you could run out of unused new ideas! You've got to keep your unused new ideas up to maximum stock level. Maybe we just get a sense of security from at least *knowing* we have good ideas.

Once we have forgotten them all or the gauge falls below a certain point we panic. So we race out and gather new good ideas – we may read a new book, go to a seminar or take a training course. Then we relax again into our comfort zone and enjoy that false sense of security that 'well at least I have unused good ideas'. The fact that we never implement them doesn't seem to matter!

I promise you that reading this book will provide you with new ideas and possibly the odd paradigm shift. But I don't want you to read it just to get your unused-new-idea-ometer's needle up! On the contrary, I want you to use the new ideas.

Therefore if you are going to read this book in the bathroom – don't continue. If you are going to read it during traffic jams on the way to work – stop now. If you are going to read it 'when you get the chance' – forget it. If you are going to read it at the beach – don't. If you are going to read it while the kids are screaming around the house – don't buy it.

Of course . . . if you've got this far then you've already bought it!!

If you sit and read this and nod occasionally and perhaps even enthusiastically – that's great for me. If you discuss the validity of some of the arguments over coffee with friends – that's great for me. But none of these avenues of expression take you anywhere different – that is not what I want.

I genuinely want this book to take you somewhere different rather than just give you new ideas.

The emphasis therefore is on turning ideas into action. In my experience gleaned from working with so many businesses, this critical character trait of turning ideas into actions is not automatic. It must be coached. People usually read very passively – simply moving their eyes over the words. They don't ever really intend to do anything different as a result. Even the environment where you choose to read something indicates how serious you are about implementation . . . Where are you reading this?

> **Do you need to know the theory and practice behind power generation in order to flick on a light switch?**

Please don't make that mistake with this book. You should only read it if you suspect you will do something different as a result and that there may therefore be something of lasting value in it.

Then you must:

1. Decide when you're going to read it.
2. Book in those hours in your diary.
3. Take a clean sheet of paper (or use the note pages that have been supplied at the back of this book), a pen and start to write down your brain traffic as you read.
4. Sit somewhere that supports you intention (careful!)

Engage in what is being written and watch what appears on the movie screen in your mind. Record what appears there because it is those sparks of thought that will merge with the thinking in this book to create your own unique applications of The Thinking System and the related ideas.

What you read is important to the author, what you think, as a result of what you read is important to you.

Write that stuff down. Don't stop and debate your thoughts just record them. Then go back at the end of each chapter and flesh out your own thinking. Test the ideas that come up for you and see if they work, implement the ones that do and discard or modify the ones that don't.

Take action.

What's important about this book is not what it teaches you, what's important is what you decide to do as a consequence of that new knowledge.

As you will discover in more depth as you read on, one of life's greatest motivators is coming up with an idea yourself. By our estimation, 50% of the motivation needed to get the job done comes from having the idea yourself.

By reading and recording your own observations and thoughts relevant to your own situation you will come up with applications for the Thinking System that will take you, your business and your life to new and exciting places of increased productivity, efficiency and harmony. The power of the idea is then with it's rightful owner – you.

So let's get started . . . Check your diary and book in your first slab of 100 minutes. Red marker – *Do Not Disturb – I'm reading 'You don't think as smart as you are'!*

That time should be enough to cover the chapters dealing with human thinking and its imperfections. A similar timeslot will be sufficient for the chapters on coaching and the Thinking System.

Part Four is best attacked by devoting 60 minutes to each chapter. In order to master each of the seven chapters on the 'New Realities' you will be invited to workshop what you have learnt. Sixty minutes per chapter will allow you to absorb the material and prepare the workshop – which is set out for you.

The reason we have workshops is also explained later in more detail but application is the only way to really *get* this stuff.

And don't forget the other purely commercial reason for workshopping rather than simply reading through this book is that these actions identify talents and skills in your team. Those natural strengths and weaknesses that once identified allow you to position people and tasks accordingly for maximum effectiveness and office harmony. Therefore you can start to elevate your workforce closer to optimum efficiency.

For a business owner, being in business actually requires you to be good at competing disciplines – like the 6 Core Functions we talked about earlier.

However the solution is not to think that you can or indeed have to learn these skills but instead to understand them sufficiently (Questions to ask) and acquire behaviour (actually ask them!) that will at least give you a fighting chance.

Part two is designed to help you understand what you are up against . . .

Part Two:

THE LIMITATIONS TO PERFECT THINKING

'I think therefore I am'
Descartes

Having established that people do not perform to their potential leads us inevitably to the question why? The first and simple answer offered by most revolves around attitude, environment and opportunity (or expressions of these issues). This answer has lead to all the so-called solutions. Solutions that advocate specific remedies for each issue. But I have always been suspicious of such response, as it has always seemed too easy. And it is. Time and experience has vindicated those suspicions. The real answer to the question is in this Section. Here we discover that attitude, environment and opportunity, to the extent that they help or hinder our performance, are only symptoms of the problem . . .

8

LIMITATIONS ON OUR THINKING

Let's remember, people arrived on the Planet before Business. We invented commerce, it did not invent us. And in many ways, we are simply not made for it.

I hate to have to tell you this but . . . your ability to think is not what you assume it is. We have a number of characteristics, which in business and life in general, turn into limitations or obstacles despite being the very characteristics that make us special. In other words, the way our brains are built is in fact a major contributing factor to our performance gap.

There are those of you who would violently disagree with me over this statement and there are those of you who right now are saying to yourself: 'No kidding Sherlock – why did I buy this book!'

Think about it for a moment, we have all heard the much-bandied about statistic that we only ever use 10% of our brain. If only that were true. It can be significantly less than that, especially first thing on a Monday morning!

We are going to focus on four of the more significant challenges. I do not want to suggest that these are the only ones that are relevant (need to leave something for the sequel!), but these are the ones that in my experience matter most.

The first limitation relates directly to language. Language in this context means both verbal and non-verbal communication, the shortcomings we must address stem from the fact that language does not have a universal dictionary.

The second limitation is that no single brain can manage 'content' and 'context' at the same time – you can't be objective *and* subjective at once!

The third limitation is that emotion does not need reality. Perception is sufficient as far as our thinking is concerned. Perception equals reality. And perception is built on what we hear, see – truth or not.

The fourth and final limitation is that, over time, we think on 'automatic pilot' – giving unconscious responses when what is needed is a 'manual' response. Whilst automation is necessary for sanity, due to the sheer volume of information that bombards us 24 hours a day, they lead to mistakes, inaccurate assumptions and errors of judgment.

So is there hope? Are there techniques to help us overcome these limitations?

Yes. The first is simple awareness and the second is called the Thinking System. The Thinking System has been successfully distilled from thousands of situations in thousands of businesses. And the great news is that some of *that* knowledge is now contained here, together with techniques that you can apply to your business.

By the time you have 'workshopped' your way through the remaining Chapters, I promise you that your thinking will have improved dramatically in three distinct but interrelated ways:

You will be able to think with more clarity and precision about your business and your own desired outcomes and create paths of thought that will successfully take you to your desired destination.

You will be able to understand, use and apply the specific techniques of The Thinking System, and

You will have learnt many effective and productive shortcuts born out of understanding and knowledge rather than guesswork and supposition.

And again, I purposely said 'workshopped' rather than 'read'!

9

LANGUAGE HAS NO UNIVERSAL DICTIONARY

The first limitation we face in our journey toward perfect thinking is the constraints implicit within our chosen method of communication: language. Language doesn't have universally, unambiguously understood words and phrases, where usage and meaning are consistent.

In order for us to function we need to be able to communicate with each other. In order for business to function this requirement is even more acute.

Consequently we need to be able to articulate our thinking into effective external communication so that we can convey our message and achieve our desired outcomes.

Look at it this way – you, the business owner or department manager are the server within a local area network – and all of your staff or employees represent the hardware and software in your business. Separately they are valuable but together they are exponentially so. Likewise, the real power is when we connect all the separate machines and allow them to talk to each other. For that to work, it's very important to select the right networking equipment and the right software. Each machine needs to be able to do what it needs to do and the network needs to allow them to do it. The networking also needs to allow them to work effectively together to share only the correct information and the information they require.

That's exactly what's happening in a workgroup. You've got the server, who is the business owner or department manager and you've got the different PC's, staff members, with their different competencies.

The different competencies and requirements of each machine will vary depending on the purpose for which it was brought into the business. So for example the accountant doesn't need Power-Point or Real Player and the designer doesn't need Attache finance package, but they all need Windows, which is in effect the common 'language' that allows everyone to communicate. And like with computer equipment – that requires "common unambiguous networking protocols" (or common language) in order to function effectively. Workgroups need it too: universal, unambiguous common meaning of all the words in the dictionary.

Think of language as 'networking' software for your brain. Your Brain in turn is the hardware. There are lots of different versions of the same software package called language. The 'version' we are working with here is English. The important difference is this: language software is a little bit different to real software. If I buy a copy of Windows and load it on my machine and yours, then if I put the same information in both, I can confidently anticipate the same *outputs* for any of the same *inputs* because it's always processed the same way.

But that is not the case with 'language' software. In fact the only thing you know for sure when two people agree on something is that they have two slightly, or very different perceptions of what they have agreed on. Test this yourself: how long has it been since you asked somebody to do something for you, they said they had done it, you asked them to show it to you and you almost whip-lashed back in disbelief when they showed you what they had done.

Imagine the scene . . . I ask Karen to do something.

John:	'Karen, have you done that?'
Karen:	(*Optimistically*) 'Yes, I've done it.'
John:	'Where is it?'
Karen:	(*Uncertain*) 'There it is.'
John:	'Where?'
Karen:	(*Confused*) 'There.'
John:	'Where?' 'There.' 'This? This is it?' (Picking it up) 'This? This is it?'

Feeling a little de ja vu? I thought you might, but just imagine on this particular occasion that Karen says, 'Well John, I suspected that there might be a bit of confusion so I took the liberty of actually recording what you asked me to do'. Karen presses the 'play' button on the Dictaphone containing the recording of my instructions. You know what I'm going to hear don't you . . . a clear description of what I am looking at. What I *communicated* and what I was imagining were *not* the same. Therefore Karen had only the ambiguous and insufficient words to work with.

Language does not have a universal dictionary. There is no universal, unambiguous common meaning to all words, *and* . . .

We know that '*a picture paints a thousand words*'. Yet we don't have the opportunity to use pictures and so we have to use words, thousands of them. Unfortunately when we communicate with each other, we never even get close to using the full thousand. In fact, I would suspect that we 'deploy' less than 100.

> **All we need to remember is that words connect to pictures and that means the 'dictionary' your target audience is using is more important than yours!**

Everybody has a slightly different interpretation of the same word. In fact everybody's definition or vision for every word, is based on their history, their knowledge, their experience and their personality – the shortcuts to understanding that have evolved through experience. And since no two histories are the same, no two dictionaries are the same either. No wonder that, as I pointed out before, the only thing that we can be sure of when two people agree on something, is that they've agreed on two different things! The problem is, that in order to do things 'perfectly' as a team, we need a common language with which we can communicate our community expectations.

Now add to this some behavioural characteristics. Imagine someone is giving instructions. The body language of the person giving the instructions is usually very animated; you'll see lots of hand movements for example. These hand movements are perfectly designed to make it very clear to the explainer exactly what it is they're explaining, but of course there's no interpretation mechanism for those hand movements or for the concentrated look of determination!

If you look at the person receiving the instructions, what do you see? Typically, you see a lot of nodding. If it's a male, you will probably see two or three times the nodding than if it's a female. I suspect this is because females have the wonderful characteristic that if they don't understand or are not sure of what's being said, they are likely to insist on more words. Whereas unfortunately testosterone forces the male to act as if they actually understand what the instructions are, despite the fact that they've got no idea. Sometimes they feel compelled to act as if they understand the instructions *even before they are given.* (Please! No letters)

So what you end up with is a lot of nodding that slowly builds to a crescendo of 'ah-ha, yeah, I get it, no problem, leave it with me,' which is closely followed by thinking 'what the hell was that all about?'

And finally as if it weren't complicated enough, in business we often actually go out of our way to cover up the true meaning of our communication.

Now lets look at these individual challenges so we get really clear on their implications.

1. DIVERSITY OF UNDERSTANDING

We all speak and *think* a different dialect of the same language, a different version of it, depending on our background, upbringing, parents, environment, education, school and a million other factors that affect our use and understanding of our language.

Here is an example, I've got three different clients who each use three very different words to describe success – 'Awesome impact on the bottom line', 'phenomenal impact on the bottom line', and 'scary'. That's how three different CEOs refer to the outcome they are all looking for. One says scary, one says awesome and one says phenomenal. If I used the 'scary' word with the 'awesome' guy he may get confused because his thought process takes him to a completely different place when he hears the word 'scary'. The result is he may end up thinking, 'is John suggesting I should be scared of this rapid growth?' His use and application of that word is completely different!

I know you're thinking that a big ugly CEO should not be effected by such a simple choice of words, but then you miss the point. Let's get our first glimpse of the Thinking System. Let's say I have a 'label' that I attach to a perception of my business when it is going really well. Let's say that the label I use is the word 'awesome'. That word then acts as a connector to that place in my thinking. What happens then if you use a different word to label that mental picture? If *you* use a word like (say) 'scary' to describe *my reality* – then think of the *thinking* that I have to go through to get to the meaning of *your* expression:

My thinking goes something like . . . 'Surely he doesn't mean scary as in "The Texas Chainsaw Massacre", and we are talking about my business so maybe he's using the word scary in a different context . . . it's probably a word that can be used to describe a good outcome . . . in fact its probably some modern expression that means "great" . . . you know like kids these days use the expression "That's sick" to mean "that's really good"' . . . and so on and so on.

Note that these types of thinking chains 'happen'. We don't decide to have them.

Note that they are triggered by others, not ourselves.

Note that they occupy one hell of a lot of time in our day.

It doesn't matter how quickly this thinking happens, it dilutes the quality of the thinking that follows. Now apply a multiplier to this equation, then ramp it up for each person in the equation. You start to see what we are up against.

> **All we need to remember is that words connect to pictures and that means the 'dictionary' your target audience is using is more important than yours!**

I am aware that there are sciences that deal with this exclusively. All we need to remember is that words connect to pictures and that means the 'dictionary' your target audience is using is more important than yours!

So whether you are running a small business or managing a department, one quick look around the office will remind you of just how different all your PC's (people) are. You hire people with very diverse skill sets and when you hire people with diverse skill sets you are also hiring people with very diverse personalities. So the person who has chosen to become a bookkeeper is by definition going to have a very different personality from the person who has chosen to become a salesperson.

The thing is that every interaction they have with each other reminds them of the differences and that's why the tools that we will discuss in Part Four are so effective. They change the balance: Instead of constantly reminding each other how different we all are, using these tools reminds them how much we still have in common . . . it brings people (or, better yet, thinking) together.

Nevertheless one of the big challenges that business owners and managers have is that we have to have people with diverse personalities in order to fill the necessary positions within the workgroup. Yet every time they interact they can cause each other some discomfort and that's why getting a harmonious and efficient office is so difficult.

In our experience the only way it can be achieved is when you have a workgroup that believes in the greater cause and that's what makes the successful business stand out. The good businesses are businesses where the outcomes the *business* promotes, those expressed in the services they provide or the goods they sell, have elevated themselves above and beyond the needs of the individual.

2. A PICTURE PAINTS A 1000 WORDS

As I pointed out before, despite accepting the truth of the phrase a "picture is worth a 1000 words", we paint our communication pictures on a daily basis with a fraction of that number. The result is a situation where people every day interact and can often miss the entire point of their interaction.

At best we use 70–100 words per picture, which means there are between 900–930 words that we leave the other party to make up!

And they do. They will fill in the gaps in our language, but what they do is they fill them in based on *their* experience, shortcuts, skills and knowledge not on *our* experience, shortcuts, skills and knowledge and certainly not on a universally accepted and collectively acknowledged platform for communication. Hence the confusion.

Add to that the fact that we all have different inter- pretations to words and those words have different meanings in different contexts and you have the makings of very poor communication indeed.

This principle is demonstrated by the old trick that motivational speakers and others have used many times. They get somebody to look at a picture that they *don't* show the audience. They ask this volunteer to describe the picture to the audience. The objective is to describe the picture in such a way that the audience can actually perceive it or re-create it.

What happens is that when people look at and compare their re-creation to the picture being described, there is very little resemblance. And that's because a picture needs thousands of words to be fully described and even those words have, as we have discussed, different meanings to different people and so it is virtually impossible to do this without talking for weeks!

So, as a rough analogy, think of the brain as a computer, and your native language as the software. Software on it's own is useless however, so we need to load data. An accounting package is useless without the numbers. A word processing package is quite useless unless you start to enter text. Your brain in this analogy relies on your life experience as data like the numbers in an accounting package and the words in a word processor. In order to deliver an outcome of value, you actually have to provide it directly, consistently and very specifically in the language that the brains of others also understand without ambiguities yet based on your own life experiences as data.

And this is almost impossible!

3. HIDDEN COMMUNICATION

The other characteristic in conversation is that we are minimalists and we communicate by body language and many other nuances such as tone and accent on particular words.

Take body language for example. You can gauge (or guess) a mood, an unsaid response and a level of enthusiasm from body language without the person uttering a single word. The impact of this type of non-verbal communication is so strong that you can feel when something is not right. It's hard to tell which is the greater of two evils though, the fact that we use these indicators to qualify the communication or the fact that we think our interpretation of them might be right! I have had many experiences where I totally misread the body language, and the outcome can lead to anything from a misunderstanding to a jail term! How many times have we been in a situation where the words being spoken are not congruent with the messages being transmitted through body language? And much as we would like to we simply cannot dismiss it as being an important part of the message. For example how many times have you asked someone to stay late at work and they have said "Yes" but their body language is screaming "No"!

Because the transaction rate in discussion is so high we are always on the lookout for shortcuts in our explanations. And we will interpret the nuances of body language – often at an unconscious level – to allow us to do that.

Lets look at how these three factors conspire against us. We'll use a real situation, which, although not connected with it, arose while Karen and I were working on this book together. It illustrates perfectly all three of the previous pitfalls!

I wanted her to do an audio production job for me and this was the start of the discussion . . .

John: I want you to produce an audiocassette.
Karen: 'Uh huh'
John: Can you do that?
Karen: 'Sure'.

I knew that Karen had some experience working in the audio production industry, hence my question. Enter Major Challenge One – our interpretation of "produce an audio cassette" was wildly different as we found out. Add to this Major Challenge Two – every time she made a positive statement or response, I used fewer words in explanation – I painted less of the picture. And finally the last nail in the coffin of our understanding was her body language – which was very relaxed and laid back, so I assumed she knew what she was talking about.

So within the space of minutes Karen had accepted the

project and all she knew was the name of the interviewees!

We happened to be writing a Chapter for this Book when the above conversation came up as an aside, so we decided to 'unpack' our interaction just to see how guilty we were of breaking our own rules . . .

John: 'Think of the job you just agreed to do. You've built a bloody clear picture in your head of what we're talking about – what are the chances that picture is anything like my picture?'

Karen: 'Umm – probably nothing like it . . .'

John: OK let's start again . . .

John: 'I want you to produce an audio cassette.'

Karen: 'What do you mean produce? What's the role you'd like me to play?'

John: 'Well, I've got the people I need to be interviewed, but I'm concerned about the fact that we'll get hung up on the discussion and not be objective. I need somebody to represent the listener there, because the audio technician's can't and the interviewees certainly will not be objective about the topic.

Karen: 'So what you're saying is you want somebody to direct and edit the recording as well as produce the tape.

John: 'Well, yeah.'

And away we go . . .

This is just a snapshot of the conversation but I hope you can see how things can so easily go wrong. One simple word, two very different impressions of its meaning and a little misread body language thrown in.

Every time she gave me an affirmative response in the first instance I would start to delete words about what I specifically wanted because I had chosen to interpret her positive and relaxed body language to mean that she understood the challenge.

> **Language has the potential to be a precision instrument to be wielded with power and clarity but in the face of these restrictions and the many anomalies it often degenerates into a blunt, lazy and altogether clumsy communication tool capable of mass confusion and widespread frustration!**

The truth is Karen could have been thinking about what she was going to have for dinner that night for all I knew, yet I was lulled into a false sense of security by her responses and her matching body language. And she was lulled into a false sense of security by assuming that I might actually know the technical difference between directing and producing! Would it have been any wonder then if I were stunned into silence when she came back with something I might not have even recognised? It didn't happen only because we applied some thinking to correct it – but it could have easily been a disaster.

Both parties have to take responsibility for giving and receiving accurate and specific detail, because the fact is, Karen's view of the world is very different from mine. But if we understand that and work towards precision then we are moving toward perfect thinking.

To quickly illustrate this, ask 5 people what their definition of 'a lot of money' is. You will be amazed at the range that statement has in actual dollar amounts. For some it may mean $10,000 for others it may mean many millions of dollars!

Language has the potential to be a precision instrument to be wielded with power and clarity but in the face of these restrictions and the many anomalies it often degenerates into a blunt, lazy and altogether clumsy communication tool capable of mass confusion and widespread frustration!

The delicate balance between understanding and confusion is much the same as the accuracy required to make the Internet work for you. The Internet *demands* precision – if you type in the Internet address and you get one letter wrong, or one full stop wrong, or one space wrong it doesn't work. The computer doesn't go 'well I think I know what you really meant' and take you to your destination; the computer is just not programmed to be able to do it.

We've convinced ourselves that our thinking is a bit more adaptive than it truly is. It's almost like we assume that quality thinking is instinctive. Running might be instinctive, but being a Gold Medal athlete requires commitment and dedication, basic thinking is instinctive but high quality thinking requires training (and just like for the athlete, the best way to achieve that is through coaching)!

4. POMPOSITY OF BUSINESS COMMUNICATION

The final hurdle rests in the very specific type and style of communication that has been created within business. In many cases 'business communication' has become an oxymoron! It is almost like we have developed this one-dimensional, flat and convoluted way of speaking to one another. The apparent purpose of which is to devolve responsibility and increase complexity to diminish understanding. The legal profession is the pinnacle of this bull but it permeates just about every corporate memo and business letter ever written.

Take the following two contrasting examples:

'It has come to our attention that the pre-agreed employment hours as stipulated by your contract are not being met. Indeed it would appear from information gathered that this agreement is being consistently and flagrantly dishonored. Please desist from this behaviour immediately otherwise the company will have to follow the official channels to take steps to rectify the situation.'

As opposed to . . .

'You have been late 4 out of 5 mornings for the last three weeks. Fix it or you'll be sacked'

Now irrespective of union rules etc. – they both mean the same thing but the first is dressed up in jargon and innuendo rather than the plain honest truth.

For some reason business hangs on to passive tense like George Hamilton hanging on to his sunbed! Passive language is weak, evasive and safe as it allows the writer to wrap up his or her message in meaningless drivel. God forbid that business communication should elicit action! Stand tall damn it, throw back your shoulders, take a deep

> Basic thinking is instinctive but high quality thinking requires training – and, just like for the athlete, the best way to achieve that is through coaching

breath and make your communication sing. Stop hiding behind the apron of the passive voice. If you have something to say, say it with conviction and clarity or don't say it at all.

So on top of all the language challenges that we mentioned earlier, the cherry on top of the cake is the fact that in business, more often than not we are trying to disguise what we are trying to communicate in a way that the writer assumes will placate the reader. More often it will also confuse and mystify him.

What a combination . . . Is there a cure? Well almost. There is a simple formula to reverse this problem, and it is easy to apply. This is how it works:

TALK THE WAY YOU THINK

Most of the communication gap lies in the fact that we talk differently to the way we think. Our instructions, demands and expectations are usually given as conclusions, when they were inspired by a series of preceding observations or experiences. The fact is if you communicate the thinking *behind* your conclusions expectations and or demands, you may not have to *make* them.

Remember Karen and my miscommunication with the audiocassette? I asked her to do the last thing I thought of rather than sharing with her the thinking that preceded the request.

I should have said something like:

'We are recording an audio cassette for business, the people being interviewed know their stuff but I am concerned it will degenerate into jargon and miss the mark for the audience. I figure that you know this audience well and you could probably pick us up if we disappear into a maze of pet topics and irrelevancies, maybe you could even guide the questions a little'.

This was the *thinking* that led to my *thought*, which was to ask Karen to produce the audiocassette. Had I given her this thinking instead of the thought she probably would have responded to my request that she *Produce* it, with 'Sure John, I'll *Direct* it!'

I have observed that effective leaders in business have this characteristic – of giving their thoughts. This way the picture is being painted in the mind of the audience.

Try it. The next time you are about to bark some instructions. Think instead of the thinking that preceded those instructions, the thinking that led you to want to give the instructions in the first instance and share those instead. You'll be surprised at the outcome.

Something else to think about:

Communication is ultimately about people. It is about getting your message across to someone else, allowing him or her to understand you. Yet we have devised way upon way to circumvent human contact. The fax machine, e-mail, voicemail, answer machines, SMS messages, on-line messaging facilities like MSN Messenger and ICQ.

And in our haste to embrace the new technologies something strange is happening to us. Cushioned from reality by a machine, that anonymity is giving us 'courage' to express ourselves more openly than ever before. But that same anonymity is removing any sense of accountability for that communication.

Its almost like we forget that we are actually communicating with real people! So whilst we feel a sense of liberation and freedom of expression it is often not tempered with humanity. And although new technology has given us new mediums to increase our communication, the quality and depth of that communication has in fact decreased.

E-mail for example can become e-vil when we replace the carefully crafted letter penned with focus, intelligence and forethought by the blunt, sterile corporate missive. We are having conversations by SMS messenger in a bastardized English that is fast becoming it's own language. We call our insurance company and spend twenty minutes punching numbers on the phone pad before we even get close to a real person!

It may all be seen as progress but what is it doing to us as human beings?

10

CONTENT VERSUS CONTEXT

Have you ever had a scalp massage? It's wonderful. Have you ever tried to give yourself one? It just isn't the same. This may explain why so many of us are so aggressive in our hunt for a partner!

On a serious note, in our problem solving we usually go along with the concept that the 'answers lie within'. And they do. So why can't we seem to extract them when we need them? The scalp massage conundrum points us towards the real answer.

Have you ever been out with a group of your friends and someone shares a problem with the group. Suddenly they are being bombarded with possible solutions. Or have you ever been thinking something over and you can't see the wood for the trees yet someone will ask you about it and as you try to explain the problem a solution will appear – as if by magic!

> **Content Versus Context is the fundamental limitation ignored by the business improvement industry.**

The problem invariably is that in order for our thinking to function to its potential, the *information* needs to be retrieved in a manner that serves the *conclusion*. Not in a manner that serves our *personal* attachment to various *pieces* of information. And this requires the one thing we can't give ourselves – objectivity.

The Macquarie Dictionary says (my emphases is underlined):

Ob-jec-tive. n. **1.** an end towards which efforts are directed. – adj. **2.** Gram.denoting the object of transitive verbs.

3. underlined{unbiased}. 4. of or pertaining to objects. – objectivity, n

Sub-jec-tive. adj. underlined{belonging to the thinking person rather than to the object of thought} (opposed to objective)

Content Versus Context is the fundamental limitation ignored by the business improvement industry.

And consequently this is the beginning of a completely different perspective on what it takes to reach your potential

Have you ever faced a challenge, and no matter how many times you go at it, you just couldn't find a solution? Then from no-where something external triggered a whole new thought process and the solution emerged.

What actually happened was your brain telling you, in the only way it could, that it was not able to do what you want it to do. It took the external trigger to remove the log jam.

There are two things required to produce your best thinking – *context*, which is what you think about and *content*, which are the thoughts themselves.

Context requires objectivity. Trying to give yourself objectivity is a little bit like deciding whether to drink and drive when you're pissed. Think about it . . . you ask a room full of people 'Is drink driving a good idea?' and the resounding response would be 'No, it's a stupid and irresponsible thing to do'. However ask the same room full of people 'who has done it?'

Apart from maybe a couple of people who genuinely haven't done it – the majority of adults have done it at least once in their lives.

So if we all agree that it is a stupid idea, why are the vast majority of us guilty of it at some point in our lives? The answer is that we made the decision when we were not in a position to *decide*. We didn't have objectivity.

Ask yourself the question why marriage guidance counselors get divorced? Because they can't give themselves the one thing they can give their clients and that is the umpire's impartial (objective) perspective.

When you visit a psychologist or a counselor, they provide context – you provide content. But when a business owner writes their own business plan, they're trying to provide both content and context. That is why training courses deliver such a small fraction of their potential value, because they are trying to cover both content and context.

Any workgroup that creates a strategic or operational plan from within are committing themselves to an outcome that is less than they are truly capable of delivering. You can only get the rest with objectivity.

The issue is the impact this dichotomy has on our thinking. In order for a thought to be perfect, two contributions must happen concurrently. Subjective skill, knowledge and experience matched with the objective, dispassionate, uninvolved questioning. The more dispassionate and uninvolved the objectivity, the more pure the thought, and the more powerful the outcome.

Imagine a stranger asks you a question about some aspect of your business. Your response is to search for the answer. Now imagine a colleague asks you the same question, chances are your defenses will rise and you will ask yourself why you are being *asked*. Look at the following statements and read each one out loud, putting the accent on the highlighted word:

Why did he ask me that question?
Why _did_ he ask me that question?
Why did _he_ ask me that question?
Why did he ask _me_ that question?
Why did he ask me _that_ question?

Your response is being affected by the fact that a colleague is asking you the question. And note that this chain reaction occurs before any thought is given to the actual answer! This is the power of context versus content. An outsider can provide objectivity and context allowing you to supply the content without suspicion, resentment or fear of polluting the process.

Let's accept a simplistic picture of the mind – I'm not a biologist or psychologist, so don't take me literally – divide the mind in two: conscious and subconscious. Your conscious mind thinks linearly – one thought at a time. Women reading this book I know will contest this. It is true that women multi-task better than men but it is the switching across threads of thought that creates that ability. The mind is still only capable of one thought at a time.

The subconscious mind thinks of lots of different things, and there is a connection between the two. In order for you to think effectively, you need to have a *context* into which all the data or *content* is placed to distil the highest quality idea you're capable of.

When content meets context

I had a client who had a number of objectives emerging from a coaching session. One of these was to write a book. As his business and personal coach I would meet with this client on a regular basis to track his progress.

We had broken down the steps to writing a book to the smallest possible components. In fact it got to the stage where all that was required by my client in the thirty days between our meetings was to suggest ten chapter headings for this book that, according to him, he had "already mentally written".

You wouldn't believe the lengths we went to in trying to make this happen. We had even agreed he would place a dictaphone in the bathroom so that there would be a moment when this individual could without any effort just pick up the dictaphone and talk when there was probably not much else to do!

Eventually at a review session, we were going through his personal plan. Before we turned to the page listing the action step for writing the book he said 'Stop, don't turn the page, I've decided I'm not an author – some *other* bastard can write the book'.

What coaching gave him was help in clarifying what he *really* wanted. I provided him with the context in the form of the 'process' he was committing himself to, he simply added his own content and eventually came up with the conclusion that he didn't want to write the book at all. Had he not had the context he would probably have gone through his entire life lamenting the fact that he had never written "that book", instead of realising that he could die happy without *ever* writing a book. It was simply not that important for him and so he was able to finally let it go.

What about movies? Imagine you're alone in the house, you've just heard on the news that a madman has escaped from a prison about fifty kilometres from you. It's midnight and there is a storm outside. You decide to watch *Silence of the Lambs*. Is that going to be a different experience to watching the exact same movie in broad daylight with half a dozen friends and you've just finished watching *The Life of Brian!* You bet it is!! It's the same movie but the context has changed *everything*.

Another great example of the content/context seperation involves sporting contests. You have the rules, which are the context, and you have the players, which are the content. In order for the game to work everyone must know the rules but rules can be broken in the heat of the moment so we have a referee, who is the guardian of the context.

The referee is the objective filter for the game and must observe the game without bias, as soon as s/he has a personal stake in the outcome their involvement is flawed. Objectivity is dissolved by emotion.

The clear difference between objectivity (context) and subjectivity (content) is that from an objective position, you can actually determine the extent to which the idea is being fueled by emotion. Going back to the rugby game – if you have no particular attachment to any one side you can observe the game from the purity of the rules and the game. Many people say they even enjoy the experience of watching two teams they *don't* support play versus watching their favourites play. The key difference is that in the second scenario – the result matters! But it's still the same game.

When you are not emotionally involved in the outcome you can appreciate the game for it's own simplicity but as soon as your side is playing, all of that objectivity flies out the window and you become obsessed, obnoxious and loud! (Author describing self!)

The same is true with the Thinking System and coaching. The coach is the guardian of the context and what a good coach will do is provide you with the template for thinking which is the context and then you 'insert' your own individual content to allow you to draw the necessary and right conclusions for yourself and your business.

A word of warning . . .

You only have to look at the number of people each year that are 'lost' to cults and fringe groups all around the world to realise the incredible power of context. We can all sit at home on a cozy winter's evening and struggle rationally with the question: what happens to seemingly normal people that they would sell their worldly goods and give their possessions to some people who are waiting for the aliens to arrive? Are those people mad? Do they have a medical condition? Perhaps they were just very unhappy? Or maybe they had a traumatic childhood?

Well, even if the answers are yes to most of those, the explanation is elsewhere, in the hands of those who take advantage of them. The way they take advantage is by controlling the 'context'. If you control information flow and only release the information that supports a particular reality – then it is very easy to make people believe in and/or question just about anything!

For these people, what they have come to believe is obvious and completely rational and it is us who are living in a fantasy world. That is the power of this concept. Ask the right question, introduce doubt, control the information, and sooner or later your reality *will* change.

Be very careful about who you allow to mess with your context!

The difference is as simple as this. You attend a dinner party with friends. They share a problem with you that appears to them complex and challenging, and may even be very personal. You almost explode with possible solutions for them. Of course, you have forgotten that a year ago you had the same problem and could not *dig* yourself out of it!

Or how about when you have someone come to you with a problem, you ask a handful of questions in an effort, in the first instance, to understand their challenge. Half way through one of *your* questions they stop you and say enthusiastically, 'stop, thanks, I know what to do, I appreciate your time.' And, as they skip away into the sunset you're thinking to yourself 'Well, I solved it. I have absolutely no idea what "it" was but I solved it!' Alternatively whatever I said gave the person a new perspective or idea that allowed them to solve it themselves.

And it happens in reverse, when another person 'imposes' context. You know what I mean, when you are explaining a problem to someone and half way through your description of the problem you think of the solution. Here you are *creating* a context, the need for which is imposed on you by the other person's *lack of knowledge*. This in turn forces you to articulate the circumstances *so clearly* that the answer jumps out at you!

Imagine that you are travelling up into the mountains to that little log cabin the family has owned for generations, the one with the trout stream near by. You are going up to spend a

> **Did you know that there are roughly 18 hours (or two solid days) of 'air time' in a workgroup's collective heads? That is if they are responding to a 'Thinking System' it only takes that long to completely pull apart and rebuild the typical business!**

couple of days away from 'distractions' to write a business plan. You drive the car as far as the dirt road allows and you hike the last 4 kilometres to the shack. When you arrive, you open the windows and let in some fresh air. You put your fishing gear to one side. Later, after you've 'done a bit of work', you will go and see if you can catch your dinner at the stream.

You put the block writing pad down on the table and the new pencils and pencil sharpener (boy will you need that!) next to the pad and you sit down to start . . . Where? Your thoughts begin 'I'll start with a mission statement . . . no I need the team for that . . . I'll list our weaknesses . . . no think positive . . . I'll look at our top ten goals for the year' and then you get the 'big idea' –

'I know, I'll put the coffee on' So you brew the coffee and hope that by the time it's ready an obvious and clear starting point will emerge! But of course by then it's getting toward mid afternoon so maybe if you go fishing now you can catch and cook your dinner before darkness and the chill set in. Soon it *will* be dark and time for coffee and Port and you will still be close to where you started . . . and so it goes.

Now imagine the same scenario. Only, while seated at the table in the Cabin you hear a knock at the door. You open the door and standing there is . . . you guessed it . . . a Business Coach.

'What are you doing up here?' he or she asks.

'Writing a business plan' you reply.

The coach, looking at the empty note pad says: 'You don't seem to have gotten very far'.

'Yeah . . . I was just aahh "warming up"' you mumble.

'Here . . . give me the pad' says the coach. '*You* grab your coffee and sit back and let's *talk* the plan.'

So the Coach begins:

'What are the ten most critical things in your business?

How happy are you with the way they are done?

How should they be done?

Let's take this one first, what would you have to do to get it right?

Is that really the first thing?

Oh . . . this would be?

And who would do that?

Why does it have to be you?

Oh . . . they could do it instead?'

Did you know that there are roughly 18 hours (or two solid days) of 'air time' in a workgroup's collective heads? That is if they are responding to a 'Thinking System' it only takes that long to completely pull apart and rebuild the typical business! Of course this is only possible by separating content from context. The exercise above, had nobody knocked on the Cabin Door, would have taken . . . what am I writing here, it would have been *impossible!* If the test of the outcome was to produce the best possible thinking – you cannot do it on your own. Sorry. Fact. Rewind your life and start again!

Another word for objectivity applied to one's self is 'hindsight'. Hindsight is a list of *answers* that were not given the benefit of *questions* that could have been asked with foresight! You don't need to be a psychic to *know* the questions, they don't change. Context is universal, content is unique to you and your team.

This is too important to leave it here, so Part III revisits content vs context.

WORKSHOP

Think of a mistake that you have made in business recently. Why was it a mistake? What questions would have alerted you to the problem?

Cautionary Note: For all of you reading this and thinking 'I wouldn't have listened to the advice anyway' – Bull! You asking yourself a question is a completely different experience from someone else asking you that same question. You can dismiss your own questions but it is very difficult to do the same to an objective external force!

Most of us at some point in our life have gone out with someone that was patently not right for us. You kind of know it but don't really want to face it so you skip into the sunset trying to convince yourself that it will all be peachy next week. You know the logic, you know the facts, you've done the pros and cons thing and the cons are three sides of A4 and you can't think of a single pro! Yet you stay until the day your friends finally ask you 'what the hell do you see in him/her?' The light goes on and it's all over . . .

11

EMOTIONS AND REALITY ARE MUTUALLY EXCLUSIVE?

In business, rational thinking and logic are the steering wheel. Emotion is the accelerator.

The issue of emotion affects objectivity and subjectivity, but it can also present a much broader challenge for us in business.

Reality is a very subjective concept to start with. If you think about it, it is actually nothing more than perception. The event itself means nothing until the individual applies meaning to the event. And perception is largely determined by emotion.

Imagine you are sitting in traffic; you're late for an appointment and you're generally pretty pissed off. Suddenly from nowhere somebody runs into the back of your car. Now you are really mad, you jump out of your car, slam the door and storm to the back of your car armed and ready with some choice expletives!

It's your brother or your sister who ran into you.

All of a sudden the knuckle sandwich turns into – '*oh no, are you okay*'?

Emotional expression is one of our greatest strengths, however if it is allowed to become an unchallenged contributor to the decision making process it becomes our greatest weakness.

Emotions do not need facts to be triggered.

The event is the same. But the interpretation, meaning and emotions that you attached to that event have completely changed.

How often do we, in business charge into meetings with

internal knuckle sandwiches and simmering resentment that can so easily distort our judgment and affect our decision-making?

Emotional expression is one of our greatest strengths, however if it is allowed to become an unchallenged contributor to the decision making process it becomes our greatest weakness. Emotions do not need *facts* to be triggered.

The best time to apply emotion is when the facts have arrived. This waiting is impossible, however, if you are part of the problem, that is, if you are part of the *content*. You may not know the difference between emotion and reality. Thus emotions happen as part of the process of thinking, when what really needs to happen is that all the thinking should be done before the emotion is engaged.

Incidentally the ability to consistently do this is a trait of great leaders.

Understanding can so easily be warped by emotion! Whilst this can be a valuable additional kick-start to create action it is also the easiest way to manipulate.

This powerful force can also be seen in sport, as we looked at earlier. I can vividly remember being at a rugby league game, the Dragons (my team) playing Manly (the enemy!).

In this particular game the Dragons kicked a field goal from about 30 metres out with seconds left on the clock and we won the game . . . and I cried like a baby! Now let's just think about that for a second . . . a guy has kicked a bit of leather filled with air between two sticks. He happens to be wearing a white jersey with a red 'V'. Last year he was wearing a blue and gold jersey and three years from now he's going to be wearing a different jersey again. But for now he's wearing our jersey.

Yet when we won that game – I had tears in my eyes. This is not logical. If something happened to someone close to me I'd cry. You could conclude therefore that I feel as much emotional attachment to my football team as I do to my family. Obviously that is not true (I think!). Yet it shows how easy it is to trigger emotions and create an illusion.

The growth of the Personal Development Industry has shown how easy it is to manipulate and control emotion. Many of today's seminars are more akin to a Billy Graham revival meeting than a business seminar! Now I am not criticising this format because quite obviously it works for some of the people that attend. A few people do change their life as a result. But for the vast majority it does not work long term because the emotional intensity of the revival-like format cannot be sustained. There is an inevitable crash back to reality/normality (whatever that is!) as illustrated by Figure 2.

What is happening in this arena is that information is being given to participants when they are in a heightened emotional state – either through music or exercises. It is not brain washing although I think we all need our brains washed occasionally, it is simply the use of emotion to create an enjoyable 'learning' environment.

The information given and the emotion felt are very often completely separate – mutually exclusive – yet in the head of the participant the information has been attached to the 'feeling good'. Therefore recall of the material is easier yet the likelihood of implementation has actually decreased.

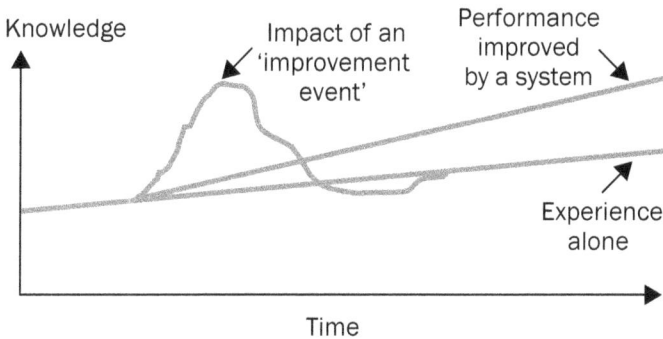

Figure 3: The difference between improvement by a special event and by a system

It's like dieting – the seaweed and grapefruit diet may help you loose 5 kg over 2 weeks but you will never maintain it. Just as seminar junkies never maintain the high! Long-term weight loss requires small and consistent lifestyle changes – not seaweed and grapefruit. You are so much more likely in the long term to implement and maintain changes that are logical and rational than those built on hype and razzmatazz.

Using emotion to engender change is the 'hit and miss' approach because we are not basing it on structured, well thought out reason that is actually relevant to the individual. Emotions can help with information recall but they don't contribute to the *translation* of the idea into action. As a result most people leave on a high and stay there for a week or so, drive their family and friends nuts with enthusiasm then realize to their dismay that they do not actually have the ability to apply or implement what their own emotions would wish. They still have the emotion but they can't apply it to their everyday life in the same way as the presenter could inside the seminar. Now it's a different emotion: anticipation soon turns to remorse.

The objectivity provided by the presenter gave perspective to the individual just as a coach will give perspective to an elite athlete. Once such a perspective is removed, the individual doesn't have the tools and skills to provide it for themselves.

As well as emotion distorting from the outside in it also has the ability to distort from the inside out. Let's revisit a previous concept. Look at the following statements we met earlier in another context and read each one out loud, putting the accent on the highlighted word:

Why did he ask me that question?

Why *did* he ask me that question?

Why did *he* ask me that question?

Why did he ask *me* that question?

Why did he ask me *that* question?

These identical sentences all instil radically different meanings, depending on the accent. The emotion associated with each sentence is also altered. For example in the first one the emotion could as easy be one of suspicion and a little fear as it could be one of boredom and indifference – it depends on your mood and feeling about the question as to the meaning that you give it. It is this kind of quirk of language that makes communication such a minefield.

The realisation that brings this issue to its fullest impact is this: emotions are actually *designed* to stop you thinking.

When you get emotional (experience fear as an example) you stop thinking and start doing: fighting or fleeing. Our ancestors 'used' fear to survive! It made them run and it made them hide. Then when they were safe, they made a spear and emerged to fight.

When dealing with someone who is anxious or concerned (emotions) you need to turn the emotion tap off before you can turn on the tap of receptivity to logic or information. That's why empathy (saying 'I know how you must feel') is a natural first response if you are trying to calm someone down.

The problem is that in most of us the emotion tap is often stuck open, as will be illustrated through the Exercise.

EXERCISE
Try this experiment.

Read the facts below, while you do – try to guage your emotions as each new piece of information is added. The story is true.

The Story of Augustine Le Prince.
- Thomas Edison was a famous inventor.
- Augustine Le Prince was not.
- Augustine Le Prince was a French inventor, who, in 1885 developed a prototype for a motion picture camera.
- In 1888 he received the first patent for a movie camera, both in France and the United States.
- He demonstrated the camera to officials at the Paris Opera House in 1890.
- Despite being well received he returned to his workshop in Leeds, England, to perfect his machine.
- Six months later he disappeared on his way to meet up with his wife, Lizzie and their children in New York to launch his now perfected camera.
- Every morgue and asylum was checked and he was never found.
- In the search for him a family friend (not realising the significance of his invention) may have destroyed vital proof of Le Prince's great achievement when he cleaned out his workshop.

How do you feel about Augustine Le Prince?
- Le Prince never patented the last design of his movie camera.
- He did however reveal his discovery to a few close friends including his patent lawyer, Clarence Seward.

- Whilst applying for the earlier patent Seward removed a crucial clause that would have given Le Prince broad protection on his invention.
- Months after Le Prince's disappearance Thomas Edison claimed to have invented the motion-picture camera.
- Seward was also Edison's patent lawyer.
- Edison's invention infringed on Le Prince's patent and despite being heralded, as a breakthrough was actually much more rudimentary than Le Prince's original machine.
- When Lizzie Le Prince tried to sue Edison she learned that under US law someone is not declared dead until 7 years after they disappear, and as long as the holder of the patent is living, only they can sue for infringement.
- Edison had a reputation for being ruthless among fellow inventors. Le Prince was at one stage going to collaborate with Edison but was strongly warned against it.
- Lizzie discovered that Seward's partner – Guthrie was in Europe at the time of her husbands disappearance.

How do you feel about Augustine Le Prince and how do you feel about Thomas Edison?

However, consider also . . .

- Inventors are often involved in patent battles.
- Whilst Edison had a reputation for being ruthless he was not known to be violent and there was no evidence to suggest a connection.
- Seward was a prominent patent lawyer of the day.
- Le Prince was an alcoholic and plagued with debt.
- We only have Lizzie Le Prince's word that her husband had perfected the camera.
- The clause that was dropped from the original application was very complicated in fact the patent office itself didn't understand it until Le prince went down and explained it to them.

So what can we conclude . . . nothing. But the information given probably engendered different feelings toward each party as you read through. This is how easily emotion is manipulated and it takes real courage to wait until all the information is in BEFORE making a decision.

(Adapted from a story in Uncle John's Absolutely Absorbing Bathroom reader by the Bathroom Reader's Institute. 12th Edition)

A simple defense against this phenomena is to ask yourself: 'Do I know everything I need to know to feel the way I feel?'

12

DEFAULT SETTINGS

You are in your car, heading to a destination that is near your home. At some point you take a wrong turn, that is you turn down a street that takes you home (your <u>usual</u> destination) instead of where you need to go at that moment. This reflex reaction is, unfortunately, not restricted to such trivial mistakes.

The final limitation I promised to consider is our use of *default settings*.

Have you ever left home in the morning and driven to work only to find yourself there 40 minutes later without remembering parts of the journey. You have driven that way so often that the whole journey is on automatic pilot. That's scary when you think how many of us are driving around in city traffic without our brains being engaged!

It is only when the way you normally go is diverted or closed for some reason that you think about what you are doing. The same is the case for much of our thinking.

Take what happens when you buy a PC. It arrives from the store and you set it up. To make using the computer easier it comes with pre-set or 'default' settings. These are things that you will come to take for granted and assume you have no control over.

Once you get more familiar with the system you will realise that within your computer there are a number of ways that you can change these default settings to be more specifically suited to your own personal requirements.

The same is true of your thinking. The default settings that inhibit your thinking are, however, developed over long periods of time. They come from parents, and siblings and they are the mechanisms that we devise over time to 'survive'.

They are the specific little quirks and habits that make us who we are. The challenge is that many of these default settings are developed through the eyes of a child and are then taken forward into adulthood and we wonder why they don't work anymore!

They are the click/whir situations where you find yourself reacting the way you have reacted a thousand times before for no apparent reason. They are the patterns of behaviour that are uniquely you, they are the specific little way you do a task, they are the habits and the 'systems' that subconsciously run your life. They are the 'but we have always done it that way'. They are the 'that won't work around here'. They are the things that you do that, if questioned about, you have no idea why. And what that has led to is the collection of system 'default settings'. These settings enable us to cope with all the decisions and information that we are constantly being bombarded with. They produce automatic responses to set situations without the necessity of thought. They are *shortcuts*!

Your default settings may be 'We've tried that before', 'the people round here won't agree . . .' 'we don't want to change anything . . .', 'it's too late for that.', 'Its fine the way it is . . .'

Default settings are thoughts that are automated, they happen without you consciously deciding to have them, and they interfere with the quality of your thinking.

But they are all necessary because without them we'd go berserk because we'd have to manage so much mind traffic. They are very much symptoms of modern life and a clear indication that more than ever before we need to have our thinking externally 'managed' through the external introduction of context. Somebody objective will always know when a default setting is being applied. Somebody subjective will not.

> **Default settings are automatic responses that 'kick in' once we have enough evidence to fit a pre-determined conclusion or point of view. We rush to them because it means we can stop thinking and either start doing or move on**

Default settings are automatic responses that 'kick in' once we have enough evidence to fit a pre-determined conclusion or point of view. We rush to them because it means we can stop thinking and either start doing or move on. (Refer to comments on how adults learn in Chapter 14.)

The most obvious example of a default setting is when you ask someone 'How are you?' Everyone replies, 'Good thanks, how are you?' What a banal thing to say yet we don't even think about it anymore – the question is asked and that default clicks 'play' and we respond like we have a thousand times before!

If someone questions you on that and says, 'Are you sure, you don't look too great', its only then, when an external force has questioned your conditioned response, that you engage in the question and answer consciously. In its simplest form that is what external interaction can give your thinking.

Go back just three generations and think about the things that people had to think about then. Now think about what we have to think about now – the difference is enormous. For example, back then they didn't have to wonder what they would wear because where they were going determined what they would wear i.e. church, factory floor, bakery. And they certainly didn't have to wonder which way to get there because there was typically only one-way to get there. And there you have the modern dilemma – you probably make more decisions between waking up and getting to work than your great great grandparents made in an entire day.

Think of it like this . . . we have, say in my case 1960s hardware that is installed at birth. Software is loaded, adapted and modified through life experience and we have been promised an upgrade for years! Each day we go out to the letterbox to check whether or not our upgrade has arrived.

It never does. And all the time the mind traffic (software) that we have to manage is increasing dramatically, while the hardware just, well . . . gets old!

Information and knowledge is growing at an exponential rate – old knowledge is combining with new to create transformations and constant growth and development.

And has the brain, i.e. the actual hardware, changed in the three generations we are talking about? No, it's exactly the same piece of biology, yet we are pumping through more information and choice and it has the potential to short-circuit left, right and centre.

It's no wonder we develop default settings but we need to be aware that we have them and assess whether they help us or hinder us?

Plus these default settings are impossible to find on your own!

Remember people will very often say one thing and mean another. It is therefore not always easy or straightforward to recognise a default setting. Only through external questioning will the truth emerge. For example if someone says 'Oh we tried that here before', an external person could then ask 'Oh really, what happened when you tried it last time?' The person will either be able to answer or you will discover that they haven't actually tried it, its become an urban myth or the experience is no longer relevant. Either way continued questioning will always get to the truth.

So, if our language is at best imprecise; our thinking is linear – making content and context converge into porridge; – if our emotions influence our thinking yet have no accountability to match reality; and if our mind has created default traps that take us to decisions before information is gathered … then no amount of 'new ways' will help bridge the performance gap! This is the crux of the problem that needs to be addressed first. And I believe to date, no one has taken this most serious of all challenges seriously!

But the solution is coming up in Part Three.

Part Three:

THE THINKING SYSTEM

A Thinking System is a set of purpose designed questions which when answered with integrity will deliver a powerful solution to a business challenge

Going through school the thought that occupied my mind was what tertiary qualification I would obtain, and therefore what faculty of what university I might apply for. I didn't think much beyond this. In the home in which I grew up, I was surrounded by parents and grandparents who took a significant interest in my and my siblings' studies. Here is a question I was never asked: 'What do you want to be when you grow up?' Here is a question that I was often asked: 'What will you study at University?'

My thinking and my choices were significantly managed by that question. It was not manipulation because I was happy to think in terms of those choices. If I were unhappy, I might have asked whether I really needed to go to uni at all. The fact remains, the questioner determines what you think about, and the responder only reacts.

This is one of the early Thinking Systems I was exposed to. That Question had a profound impact on my perception and kept active in my mind thoughts that led to a predictable outcome. The easy conclusion is that it is just a clever question. I have discovered that there is a science behind every perception and a fastest way to every solution.

The key to bridging the gap between performance and

potential begins with overcoming the limitations to our thinking – and like it or not that means managing our thinking. This technique has been used extensively by so-called 'psychics'. But they manipulate your thinking. I assure you that real Coaches only manage your thinking! That means finding thinking formulas that can bring immediate context to any thinking challenge.

The pages that follow provide a first look at those formulas – called Thinking Systems.

13

BRIDGING THE GAP . . .

So just to recap on our limitations . . . we have a fairly poor communication tool in language, we have an absence of objectivity, we have uncontrolled emotion *and* we kid ourselves that we are making informed choices when actually we are relying on often outdated and perhaps destructive default settings.

Yet this is the 'equipment' we use to run our lives and our businesses. On top of which we often don't have the experience in the individual specialist skills we need to run the business. Leading a team of people each with the same thinking challenges, hoping somehow to deliver something close to our potential.

And you ask me if making a business work is hard? No, it's not hard – it's bloody near impossible. While lots of businesses *survive*, that survival is measured against failure. If it were measured against *potential* the true extent of the tragedy of business would be uncovered.

But cheer up – the worst is over. The light at the end of the tunnel is visible – and it's not that proverbial train heading towards you!

Hopefully I have demonstrated the principal limitations that cause our thinking to be considerably less than optimal. Having your thinking as sharp as it can be is not 'optional', it's compulsory.

What would it mean to your business if everyone in the

> **While lots of businesses *survive*, that survival is measured against failure. If it were measured against *potential* the true extent of the tragedy of business would be uncovered**

business was reading the same road map in the same language and understanding the same vision – how much more effective would your business be?

How much more efficient would your business be if you could 'network' the brains of your team members?

Imagine this; on the side of everyone's head is a socket not unlike the one for the telephone cable that connects your computer to your modem. You and your staff come to work in the morning, grab the cord and plug it in, and whatever they were all thinking was communicated to everyone, in full Technicolor, straight away.

Now, let's accept the fact that if that were done, some people might end up in jail! But I ask you, would your business be more efficient? And the answer is Yes – absolutely yes because you could communicate *all* of your expectations. Also when somebody improved and changed a process or a function they would be able to see immediately what the ramifications of that change would be on the company and the people within it. They would be operating from 100% knowledge of the company as a complete entity rather than 80% knowledge of their own area.

The Thinking System is a technique that delivers a result that partially equates to this example. It provides you with 'software' that acts like an information management system. The problem is that we have always 'overstated' how unique and special our individual circumstances are. We therefore felt compelled to find a new or unique way, our own context, for solving problems.

My first two years as a Business Coach were wonderful. Every business presented a new challenge and around every corner a new set of issues to help my clients navigate their way through to a solution. Clients would tell me "Our place is a little different" and I would believe them! They would ask me if I had experience in *their* Industry because it was 'special' . . . and I believed them, often wondering whether I was truly qualified to 'help' them.

Then, almost overnight the *landscape changed completely*.

All of a sudden *nothing* was different. Nothing was new. And the "our place is different" illusion became exposed for the misconception that it really was. Think about it. Business people tell you their business is 'different', has 'special challenges'.

But how could they possibly know? How could they draw such a conclusion? They spend every day in their *own* business yet they still don't fully understand it. They have at best a cursory view of other businesses! And *their* place is *different*? I am afraid not.

For me the challenge suddenly shifted from being a case of trying to help clients find solutions (having now seen it all!) to finding quicker ways to leading them to the solution, shorter cuts. Then I worked out that the solutions (or at least the thinking behind the solutions, what we now call *content*) was almost always in the hearts and minds of my clients already. All they needed was the technique (*context* through Thinking Systems) to line up the content so that the pathway to their solutions became obvious.

It seemed that it was the outcome that they were driving towards delivering that dictated the context and *not* the business type, industry or their special circumstances. In other words the obstacles were more biological than commercial.

Then I emerged with a shortcut to the solutions and was able to charge a coaching rate for the context (Questions) instead of the pathetically high consultants' rates for the content (Answers). **Remember that clients all know the *outcomes* they want even before we arrive. Hell, they knew them even before they went into business in the first place!**

Thinking Systems are the systematic use of questions that can elevate the quality of your thinking, which will in turn elevate the quality of your communication. This in turn will lead to less frustration in the work team, a more harmonious work team and definitely a more productive and profitable work team.

And this is not unsubstantiated theory. It's practical and it works!

There is only one best thinking path to building a strategic plan. There is only one best thinking path to building an operational plan. There is only one best thinking path to decide whether or not to enter into a joint venture. There is only one best thinking path to decide whether to go into business in the first place. This is science. The answer lies more in managing the information in your head than in getting the information you need!

Thinking Systems allow all the information, knowledge and skill within to be accessible by all the people in the business.

You can learn to apply the Thinking System principles to narrow the gap between your business' performance and potential or you can employ an external business coach to close it.

The place for the Thinking System is twofold. There is the ad-hoc application of the Thinking System that develops as your awareness and appreciation of the limitations we have described develop. This allows you to apply the Thinking System *approach* to *any* challenge you have in your life or business.

Once you understand the power that lies within questions you start to think in a questioning way and this spontaneously develops into a Thinking System mentality, which will be of enormous benefit to you both in your business and your personal life. Chapter 15 deals with this application.

The second application of the Thinking System is in the structured approach. This is where various sets of questions have already been developed to address common business situations. The journey that you take through the questions depends on the answers given. This more complex approach is dealt with in Chapter 17.

While the need for Thinking Systems lies in our thinking limitations, why they work lies in some behavioural characteristics that are equally important to understand. Before unpacking these two approaches, let's look at the behaviour that is going to make it work for us!

14

PREDICTABLE ADULT BEHAVIOUR – TURNING WEAKNESSES INTO STRENGTHS

I often get asked how I started thinking about the Thinking System. What were the factors that led me towards its synthesis?

There were three important and separate observations that set me on the path to its discovery. Since we are about to turn them into *assets* through Thinking Systems, it is worth revisiting them.

The three 'Observations' are:

1. Invention is a Primary Motivator,
2. Idea into Action is a talent, not a job,
3. Adults cannot be taught

1. INVENTION IS A PRIMARY MOTIVATOR

People are highly motivated by their own ideas.

Yet this is only part of the issue because an idea is only valuable if it is translated into action. But one of the crucial indicators as to whether or not action will be taken is the source of the idea. If you get an idea then tell it to the person who is responsible for implementing it, it has a statistically limited chance of being implemented. Why? Because the person having to do the work is not personally attached to the idea. His or her ego has not been engaged by this idea.

If on the other hand the person who has to do the doing thinks the idea is his or hers, the chances of it being

> **If the person who has to do the doing thinks the idea is his or hers, the chances of it being implemented improves dramatically because turning that idea into reality is now personal and that's inspiring.**

implemented improves dramatically because turning that idea into reality is now personal and that's inspiring.

Experience has shown also that if someone is capable of having an idea or drawing a conclusion, then with some thinking help they are typically also capable of building the 'how' as well. It is very rare indeed to have a structured thinking approach lead to a strategy that the group who devised it cannot implement. But as we are about to discover, this is not an 'automatic' process.

The great news about this simple fact is that the Thinking System allows you as the workgroup leader to create an environment that takes advantage of the power of invention. One that encourages and allows people the freedom to come up with the ideas that the workgroup leader wants them to come up with. The Thinking System replaces *instruction* with *questions*. Therefore you have the opportunity with the Thinking System to harness this powerful force within your own environment and move your business forward at an alarming (dare I say scary) rate. This has side effects as well! It promotes an exciting, dynamic and fun environment for your employees too. A true Win-Win approach.

2. IDEA INTO ACTION IS A TALENT NOT A JOB

The second crucial discovery was that the ability to turn an idea into action is a talent and therefore not everyone has it. It is not a learnt skill. You can't just teach it and it is false to assume that it can be easily engendered in people. They will have the

> **I know the difference between a face that is wondering about the answer and a face that is wondering about the question – no software can do that.**

knowledge required in most cases to follow through on the idea, but they do not have the innate skill to construct that knowledge into a series of logical action steps in a context that makes implementation easy.

Come on, you *do know* this. You have people you work with who when they tell you they will do something you know that it is as good as done. Yet others who will tell you they will do something and you treat their words as a simple reminder that you are going to have to do it yourself!

We 'right this off' as application and commitment being the missing ingredient. And occasionally it is. But that is the exception rather than the rule! Fact is that the conversion process – reverse engineering outcomes into simple action steps – is a complex thinking challenge and some people just 'have it'.

For me this was one of the most important observations simply because there is an unspoken assumption by people in business that taking action is a natural and obvious thing to do. Certainly every business book and motivational speaker relies on this! Can you see that this idea – 'now that I have given you the knowledge it is up to you and your commitment' – is untrue and unfair? In fact given the chance to act or not to act most people will *want* to act – but *cannot*.

The limitations we discussed make it impossible.

Ask one of your chronic implementers what makes them able to turn ideas into action and they will most often say 'I just do it' or 'It's easy' or 'I don't understand why everyone can't do it'. This is a dead giveaway that it is a *talent*. The expression of the Art is always complex, yet the doing or creating to the artist is natural/simple. If you understand this and, more importantly, accept it then you can implement systems and processes that assist people over the hurdle between idea and action.

So we need to have a context (that word again!) that will move us forward to action and that is what the Thinking System provides. It helps to manage thinking through the creation and implementation of ideas rather than systems and procedures. It almost forces us to take the necessary next step and the next and the next – intellectually – so that it becomes easy physically. Those systems can then provide for us some accountability and responsibility for making it happen.

As a Coach I sometimes have to ask the same question four different ways before the team appreciate what I am driving at. I know the difference between a face that is wondering about the answer and a face that is wondering about the question – no software can do that.

Where do 'Do-It-Yourself' type aids fit in this equation? After all they can explicitly address content and context separately. The answer, however is mostly no.

For example you could go and buy a DIY business-planning software package that provides a system to assist you to take specific action. However you will most probably fail to take effective action with it . . .

Why?

Because the people who design and write such programs already know how to do it! *Yet for DIY to work for the majority of users, it has to be authored by someone who doesn't know how to do it.* That way the creator of the DIY process would be taking you with them on their journey as well as your journey from ignorance to knowledge. The author therefore would have to document the process as he or she does it for the first time.

This is essential and rare. It is the reason why so many DIY programs don't work. You can't un-know something once you know it and therefore the instructing process is polluted and is less effective. Because once someone knows how to do something they forget bits of how they have learned to do it in the first place, how they have progressed to their level of unconscious competence.

Imagine someone asked you to write down 'How to drive a car'. You would probably write something like this . . .

'Get in the car, put on the seat belt, depress the clutch, turn the key, take the hand brake off, put the car in gear and take your foot off the clutch'.

If a complete novice followed those instructions they would probably stall the car if they even got that far. Why? Because the depth of information you actually gave about the nuances of driving a car have moved from 'something you think about' to automatic pilot.

What a complete novice would require is something more like this . . .

'Open the car door and get into the driver's seat, which is the one with the steering wheel! Pull the seat belt out and clip it into the holder between the two front seats. Make sure the car is in neutral – to test this move the stick shift from side to side, it should be in the bar of the H. When you are sure the car is in neutral, push your foot down on the clutch. The clutch is the outside pedal – the easy way to remember that is ABC from right to left – Accelerator, Break, and Clutch. With your foot pressed down on the clutch shift the gear stick into first gear. First gear can be located and engaged by pushing the gear stick as far left as possible and pushing it up. Look in the rear-view mirror and the driver side mirror to check for traffic. When you are sure you are clear, turn the steering wheel in the direction you wish to travel and slowly let your foot off the clutch.'

Because driving a car is so second nature after a while you forget all the little, but crucial steps that you actually go through every time you get in the car.

Just as an aside – look at that last paragraph again. I actually assumed a huge amount of prior knowledge. For example how do I clip the belt on? Clip is a very subjective word . . . What's a clutch? What is neutral? What exactly do I mean by the bar of the H? The room for misunderstanding even from this seemingly straightforward explanation is massive!

Go back to the content vs. context limitation. This limitation tells us that you can't be wondering what the question should be and trying to provide the answer at the *same time*. With a do-it-yourself program where someone else is providing the question, if it is a static offering (like a software package), instead of wondering what the next question should be you are wondering what the next question means! Because language has no universal dictionary you have to somehow borrow the authors history and their dictionary to fully get it. There is no better evidence of this than the last mildly complex toy you bought your kids. I'm sure you didn't need this book to find out that the biggest lie in the world of Children's Toys is this . . . (to be read in your best game show host tone) . . . 'Just follow these simple instructions . . . '

That is what happens when someone is authoring a DIY program. When they start to explain "how to" there are huge chunks of knowledge or simply tiny little details that are forgotten or ignored and so the DIY only works for the 10% of users who happen to think in the same way as the author.

3. ADULTS CAN'T BE TAUGHT!

The great thing about kids is they know they don't know. The reason that kids ask 'why' so much is because not knowing is acceptable.

But something happens between the age of 11 and 20. Some strange biological imbalance starts to make us feel as though we ought to know *everything*! I had witnessed this biological imbalance many times, both, I hate to confess, in myself and in those in business around me, and it led me to this 'third discovery'.

My evidence for this proposition comes from my experience in the Financial Services Industry. As Education Chairman for the Industry Association I commissioned a study on the effectiveness of the courses we provided.

The Industry as a whole suffered from enormous 'churn' with very few intermediaries lasting longer than 4 years in the business. In fact the major Underwriters owned up to the fact that 90% of those who joined the Industry were gone within 4 years.

Now apart from the obvious waste of time for the inter-mediary and the Companies they represented, this inefficiency was costing the insurance industry millions of dollars in recruitment and training.

I wanted to know if our Association programs were positively impacting this statistic.

The result found that 80% of people who graduated from the Associations introductory program were still active members ten years after completion!

The study went on to investigate what was different and this is what made those programs special: they didn't actually teach anything, **they allowed the participants to learn**.

The approach the course took was 'this is your assignment for next week – try this'. The participants got the assignment on a yellow sheet of paper. Then when they came back a week later with their answers on the yellow sheet they were then given the white sheet, which provided the theory behind the actions. So basically the training forced them to learn **through experience not theory**. If you like, Adults learn backwards – which is the basis for the expression 'learn from your mistakes' because it's about the only bloody learning we grown-ups do!

I attributed the outstanding results of the survey to this approach. For me it led to the conclusion that adults would only learn through doing and having that doing interpreted.

The best way to get an adult to develop the discipline to build a business plan for example is to coach them through writing one. By creating an environment that will allow them to build the business plan as a series of answers to questions that are important to them. Not by teaching them the theory behind the planning process.

Let's say I took two business owners. One I taught the principles of a SWOT analysis and then said go away and do one on your business. The other I simply asked the right questions (context) and recorded their answers (content). The first business owner is unlikely to act on the knowledge. But the second now has the benefit that the knowledge (how to design a SWOT) is intended to deliver. Unless the first business owner intends to *leverage* their newly acquired knowledge it is useless to them. The next time they wish to apply it they will likely have to re-learn it! On the other hand, the second has the *benefit* of the knowledge, whether they understand it or not. *And* if they experience the benefit they are likely to go back and unpack it! Now they are motivated to understand and apply it.

The Thinking System can serve as a framework to engage the workgroup and take them through a natural (but not automatic!) process of thinking. Each part of the process is its own small but crucial piece of the puzzle. But by chunking it down into manageable sections that are easy to complete it becomes an adventure not a chore. And when suddenly the last piece slots into place and the picture is complete, they get to step back from that and say, 'Look what we did'. Only at the end do they realise that it's a business plan that would make a Harvard MBA proud.

> **The best way to get an adult to develop the discipline to build a business plan is to coach them through writing one.**
>
> **By creating an environment that will allow them to build the business plan as a series of answers to questions that are important to them.**

So we have 'Invention is a Primary Motivator', 'Ideas into Action is a Talent' and 'Adults can't be taught'. Why share this with you? Well, from the start, armed with these three observations, I wanted to avoid being trapped by this behaviour, or if you like I wanted to work with it rather than try to change it.

This meant creating a methodology that addressed all of them and provided a reliable path that participants could 'think' through, taking them from idea to ownership, action and learning via a tried and tested system. One that led them to *their* outcome through a series of experiences/actions that they could claim as their own.

And that is exactly what a Thinking System does. It gets you to connect with *your* idea to create primary motivation – it provides a framework where you can systematically turn that idea into action and engineer the outcome. And it does that through focusing on what needs to be done instead of getting bogged down with the theory or technicalities of why it needs to be done.

There is a range of Thinking System applications, from trivial to complex and *very* weighty. The range of its application in itself illustrates the power of the technique.

Obviously the pre-structured applications tend to be more complicated and work best with a trained facilitator, however the ad-hoc application is still very powerful. They are devised to overcome the four limitations in our thinking, and to work despite the three behaviours we have just visited. It's time to unpack them.

15

THE THINKING SYSTEM

The best thinking needs the best *content*, and the only way to maximise the content is to have the best *context*. The person or people providing the content *cannot* simultaneously provide the context.

Content is subjective, what I know. Context is objective, what should I think about *next*?

While the context is driven by the *outcome*, the individuals who will benefit from the outcome drive the content.

Because outcomes are universal, so is context. Because people are unique, so is content.

Let's say you and I both need to live in a comfortable environment. Assume we are both about to think through some strategies to make our environment match our needs. Let's say that comfortable for me is hospital standard cleanliness. Yes folks, I am the guy who needs to wipe the ring of water left by the bottle of beer off the coffee table before I can sit back and look over the coffee table towards the TV without having a stress attack! Let's say that you are normal, and need an environment that is 'lived-in'.

> The best thinking needs the best *content*, and the only way to maximise the content is to have the best *context*.
>
> The person or people providing the content *cannot* simultaneously provide the context.

To get our respective environments right requires the same *context* despite our differing *content*.

83

To achieve this our first question might be, 'What makes you comfortable?'

Let's say our answers are different. I might say 'to be comfortable I need hospital standard cleanliness', you on the other hand may say 'lived-in'. Despite that the next question is the same.

Based on the above information, 'What is it about your current environment that does not match your needs?'

Again, regardless of our answers to that question, the *next* question is the same, 'What prevents you from changing those things to bring them into line with your needs?'

The answer will point to something unique to each of us, and expressed 'individually'. For example 'I would not be allowed to change my environment in line with my needs' – really means 'no control'. 'I have to consider others' really means no control. In a no control situation the next question is the same, 'What stops it from becoming your choice or allowing you influence over the decision?'

> There are a million different potential joint ventures. There is only one approach when the parties enter the room.

Note that there are a million different ways to say, 'I don't have control'. But to the Thinking System expert the responses are limited. No control, no desire, no money.

Something within tells us this is too simplistic.

You want to think that it might be that easy only when you confront a simple and perhaps not so life threatening challenge – like arranging your living room. Does it get more complex, like with say a business plan for a Joint Venture between three Major Financial Institutions? No.

When I had three representatives from three major Financial Institutions in the room to negotiate a highly market sensitive joint venture opportunity, I was counselled by them how long the process would be, how sensitive it all was.

It took less than 60 minutes to get the issues on the table. It took exactly one day to exhaust the discussion and set the research parameters. In two weeks the research was done. It took one more day to agree on the terms and variables. It took 70 days from start to finish to get sign off from three Boards of

Directors in their three different languages with their three different sets of protocols!

Here is a sample from that experience. At the start of the day they looked nervously at each other. So I asked this question, I picked one of the Companies representatives and said this. 'Point to one of the other parties in this room and finish this sentence', 'the only circumstances under which we would contemplate moving forward with you are . . .' The exercise was repeated and within minutes an Agenda authored by the team was in place. There are a million different potential joint ventures. There is only one approach once the parties have entered the room.

Content is unique: Context is universal! Tattoo those words on the inside of your eyelids . . .

Let's build this from the ground up.

Remember we discussed in the early chapters the concept of 'talking backwards'. This meant sharing the thinking behind your thoughts, before the thoughts themselves. Hopefully you may even have had an opportunity to try it out.

Let's revisit how that works, now that we know it forms the basis of a Thinking System.

Say a very important client, Joe Smith, is visiting your business.

You want the team to clean up the office and make it look presentable for Joe's visit.

Why?

Because Joe represents 20% of your turnover, has an influence on other customers and you want to remain profitable.

In most cases a business owner might simply say 'Hey gang let's clean the place up.' (That is the communication begins with the thought – not with the thinking.)

If we apply our 'talking backward' technique we would say something like this:

'Hey gang, Joe Smith is visiting us next week. He is an important customer with 20% of our business going to his companies and a fair bit more of our business is indirectly influenced by him. We need to make an impression so I want this place looking ship shape.'

Now, you don't have to be Einstein to work out that the second communication will make a big difference. The request has been communicated in more words and has thus painted more of a picture. The priority has been made indirectly clear and there is a disguised benefit in the form of 'we all get to keep our jobs if we make Joe happy'!

Now, each of these ideas or facts can be turned into a question, a type of Thinking System where you want to drive towards a *particular* conclusion:

Let's examine what might happen if you were to apply the Thinking System technique here.

You: 'Is everyone aware of what's happening next Tuesday?'

Workgroup: 'Isn't that the day Joe Smith is coming to visit.'

You: 'Does everyone know who Joe Smith is?'

Workgroup: Mumbling from the group . . .

You: 'Graham, you're the man on the money can you just share with the rest of the group who Joe Smith is?'

Graham: 'Joe Smith is our biggest client and accounts for 20% of our income!'

Workgroup: 'Oh . . . Ah . . . Eeeh!'

You: 'Are we clear, folks, on what we are hoping to accomplish with Joe Smith's visit?'

Workgroup: 'Well we want to make sure that it's positive and effective'.

You: 'So what do we need to do to make sure his experience is positive and effective?'

Workgroup: 'We should put a welcome board up'.

Wow! You've asked the question instead of giving an instruction, and what you've got is an idea that you didn't have to begin with.

You: 'That's great, can we do that? Who could organise a welcome board?' (Usually the person with the idea will volunteer). 'Fantastic! What else do we need to do?'

Workgroup: 'I think we should actually put a pack together so that he can leave with something, you know, some of our new stuff, because he's a big client of Product A but I don't think that we've really brought Product B and C to his attention. I think we should put a sample pack together for Mr. Smith to take with him when he leaves.'

Benefit no. 2 that you didn't have before you asked the question! But you still have your problem – they haven't said 'clean the place up'. So you simply asked again . . .

You: 'That's great. What else can we do?'
Workgroup: 'I think one of the things we should do is make sure that Mr Smith gets to spend time with all the people that are serving his account.'

My goodness – idea no. 3. Remember that all you want is for somebody to volunteer to clean the place up. It hasn't happened yet so you ask again . . .

You: 'Is there anything else?'
Workgroup: 'We need to clean the place up. We really should make sure that reception is looking impeccable.'

Bingo! Three new ideas, plus your objective fulfilled.
You may be saying to yourself at this point, 'Yeah right John that worked well but what happens if they never give you the answer you are looking for?'

Well in 'case of emergency break glass' – remember Thinking Systems are questions. You are not allowed to say, 'clean the place up'. So here's your fail-safe:

'Do you think, folks, that the place needs to be cleaned up, or are we happy with it as it is?'

Even in that context if someone says, 'Ah I think we should give it a bit of a touch-up' it is still them borrowing a share of the idea. So they're still buying into the idea.

And you have not issued one single instruction.

'But John, this approach takes too long'.

Look . . . if you are at war and in the front line, I am not suggesting that the Sergeant gets the platoon around and says

'Listen I've got this little order that's just come down the line suggesting we retreat from this barrage, how do you men feel about that?'

The point is the time taken in my example above has lead to three ideas instead of one, has a greater chance of succeeding, and is a catalyst for positive culture. The technique requires less skill than patience and puts the right people in charge.

All you did was ask questions that triggered thinking which in turn loaded the necessary information into the mind of the people you were speaking to. Armed with that information it was only a matter of time until they concluded what you had already decided. You got the solution you were looking for. Plus it gave you a bucketload of extra bonuses on the journey.

And the System? Where is the Thinking System in all this? It is partly in the discipline of continuing to question, but largely within the purposeful selection of the very questions themselves.

From this illustration it should readily emerge that the questions making up the Thinking Systems are designed in reverse. In other words, first identify the conclusion or first identify the challenge, and then build the Thinking System backward from that point.

The system's application is clearly not limited to Business.

To illustrate this I will share a short story with you. Here's is some background; I grew up in an environment where if you made a commitment to something, you were obligated to stick to it. The only thing that could justifiably stop you was death.

My daughter becomes a Girl Guide. One night she states at the dinner table that she's not attending Girl Guides this Thursday because her friend is having a Halloween party. I, because of this commitment thing have an internal cathartic explosion but manage to control myself. So in the coolest voice I could muster I ask . . .

Father (1):   Tell me again about the Halloween party.
Daughter: Well, it's on Thursday and it's going to be at Mary's place.
Father (2):   OK. And who's going to be there?
Daughter: Well, Mary, Maria, Marlena, Melissa.

Father (3):   Tell me what happens at Girl Guides.

Daughter: Well we get together and we do a whole heap of exercises.

Father (4):   When I pick you up from Girl Guides you're normally just playing, running around.

Daughter: Yes that's at the end. In the meantime we do exercises.

Father (5):   What's the name of the lady that takes care of you at Girl Guides?

Daughter: It's not like a baby-sitting service, Dad, Jacqueline's actually a Guide Leader and she works.

Father (6):   I understand that. And she turns up and basically just sets up some exercises for you?

Daughter: No, she doesn't. When we turn up she's already decided what we're going to do and she has a plan for all of us because we're all going for different badges.

Father (7):   So she puts a fair bit of work into it?

Daughter: Yes.

Father (8):   And how many of you are in the troop?

Daughter: Eight.

Father (9):   And how many of you are going to the Halloween party?

Daughter: (after a moment's thought): Six.

Father (10):   So tell me, just out of interest – when this girl, Jacqueline you say? turns up for Girl Guides next Thursday night, having prepared for each of you to help you grow and develop and to push you on your journey, and finds that only two people have turned up. Just describe to me how you expect she will feel when she discovers you are all at Mary's Halloween party?

Long silence . . .

Daughter: I don't have to go to the Halloween party.

The key is, all I did with my questions was bring forward the facts that led me to my conclusion, in the hope that they were going to 'connect'. It was a hunch that if she were brought to some consciousness about all of those same facts she might, if her Mum and I had done the job properly over those twelve years of her life, also draw the same conclusion. And the reality is that she did.

She didn't go to the Halloween party, and when she rang her friend she actually applied the Thinking System on her friend. However it turned out her friend's parents had simply told her she couldn't go to the party.

This experience improved my relationship with my daughter. Reality is that she was never going to be allowed to go to the Halloween Party, but the decision was hers.

So Vamos – one, Marie's parents – nil! I got the same outcome but my daughter wasn't angry with me for not letting her go to the party.

SIMPLE THINKING SYSTEMS

Here's the above interaction represented Diagrammatically:

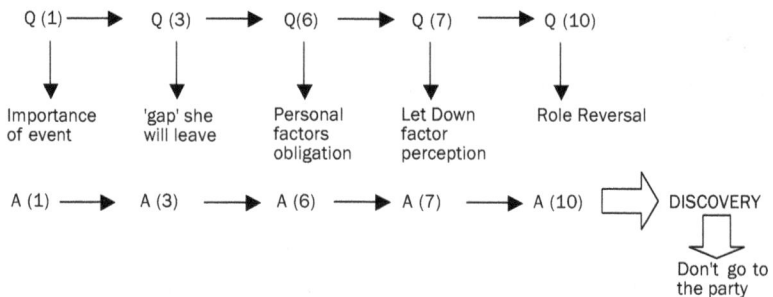

Figure 4: Thinking System in a one-on-one dialogue

I knew I didn't want her to go to the party and I also knew that if I made her aware of what I was aware of she would more than likely come to the same conclusion. So I turned my main points of argument into questions that allowed her to draw the same conclusion that I had.

Each of the arguments above could have as easily been simple statements and that approach would not necessarily have led to the discovery that I wanted her to make. This way I was enrolling her and

| Winners ask questions – losers make statements |

making her think about the answers rather than just getting defensive.

Let's look back at the Joe Smith visit.

Looking at that example again diagrammatically you can see it's just a system being played out until your answer is forthcoming . . .

So a Simple Thinking System is characterised by the fact that you know what you want to achieve, and you simply convert that information into questions. These questions when loaded into the mind of the respondent will result in that person also 'coming up' with your answer.

Complex Thinking Systems are applied when you don't necessarily know the answer but you know the outcome you are trying to achieve. We will look at these in Chapter 18.

So, identify something that's important to you that you want your team to work on, and then list all the information that's needed in order for them to be able to draw the same conclusion. Then create questions that solicit that information in the form of answers. Test it for yourself . . .

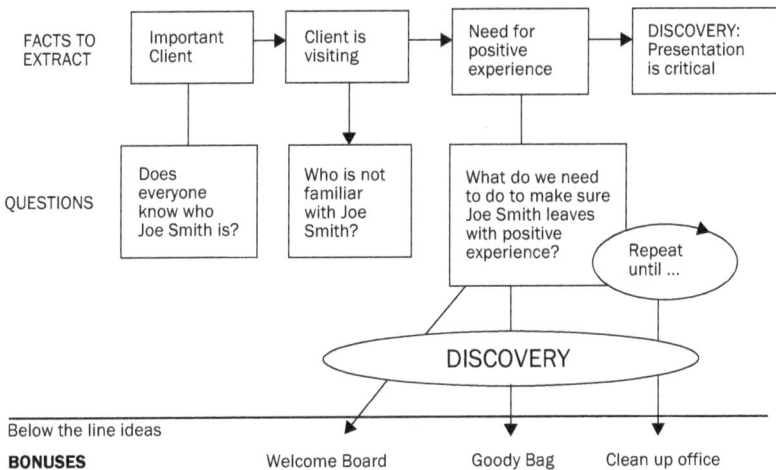

Figure 5: Thinking System in a one-on-many dialogue

16

QUESTIONS – The Heart of the Thinking System and Software For The Brain

Just because it's simple . . . it doesn't mean it's easy.

Paddy is sitting in a bar at the local pub having a slow glass of Guinness. Shamus comes in and sits next to him. Paddy turns to Shamus and asks him where he's from. Shamus replies 'I'm from County Cork', Paddy is very excited 'I'm from County Cork – barman get this man a Guinness'. Half an hour later Paddy turns to Shamus and says 'Where about in County Cork are you from?' To which Shamus replies 'I'm from Clonakilty'. 'Away, you never are – I'm from Clonakilty – barman get this man a Guinness'. Half an hour later Paddy turns to Shamus and says 'Where about in Clonakilty are you from?' Shamus tells him 'I'm from O'Reilly St'. Jumping out of his seat in surprise Paddy exclaims – 'Now that's just uncanny – I'm from O'Reilly St – barman get this man a Guinness!'

This goes on all day – the new barman comes in to take over the shift and is taken aback by the amount of Guinness that's been drunk! 'So what's been happening today?' he asks. The barman replies 'The O'Shaunessy Twins are in again!'

Remember our definition earlier – A Thinking System is a series of questions, which when answered with integrity will deliver a powerful solution to any given challenge.

A Thinking System is in fact a thought-process that captures the right information to allow the correct conclusions to be drawn. The mechanics for capturing that 'right' information is 'right' questions.

Questions are the heart and substance of every Thinking System.

Questions are everything, together with their sequence. Good questioning is beyond an art form, it is science.

Questions are the compass that will navigate even the most inexperienced traveller through the maze of their own thinking to the clarity of understanding.

If you accept the paradigm that 'you do not know what you do not know' you can release the power of questions to uncover exactly what you do know *and* discover exactly what you don't know. Through these insights you can finally unpack your own behaviour. In so doing we can create our own personal 'idiots guide' to unlock our own unique abilities, skills and talents so that their expression doesn't fall to circumstance and chance but instead becomes a repeatable system that can be 'turned on' anytime, anywhere.

We've all at some stage in our lives had someone say to us 'That's a great question'. This is the compliment all Coaches live for. Consultants perhaps hope for the statement 'Gee, that's a good idea.'

But the idea you want or need is nearly always in your head! So when the *questions* needed to achieve this are clearly thought out and arranged in a *sequence*, they become a Thinking System. But, any way you look at it they are still questions. Of course, they skillfully elicit bytes of information that need to be collected and then (as if by magic) *connected*!

Questions have a magnetic quality that pulls you toward knowledge. But just as the right question can pull you to the right answer – the wrong question can propel you in the opposite direction where you are in fact pushed away from the truth.

Again, the right answer to the wrong question is still the wrong answer.

So the challenge is two-fold: you must not only answer correctly, truthfully and with integrity but just as importantly you must *ask* correctly.

Let me illustrate this. I once attended a conference where the speaker was talking about his real estate business and how his agents would try to get opportunities from their natural market by asking –

'Do you know anyone who needs to talk about real estate today?'

This was the question members of this team were trained to ask.

So you can imagine, small town USA, all the real estate agents wore big smiley-face name tags saying 'Hi my name is X, talk to me about your real estate challenge'. Whether they were paying for their groceries or going to the drug store to buy pharmaceuticals they would say to cashiers 'Thanks Mary, do you know anyone who needs to talk about real estate today'.

The result of this approach was about a 5% positive response.

In an attempt to increase that percentage they decided to change the question and the new question was –

'Who do you know that needs to talk about real estate today?'

The new benchmark for response increased fourfold. Now it could have theoretically gone to 100% because everyone must know *someone* who they *suspect* might need to talk about real estate but still the response rate quadrupled – a fairly impressive increase achieved by a very subtle difference in the question.

So why did the percentage of positive responses increase so dramatically?

If you have had sales training you will probably be answering my question this way: 'John that's easy the first one was a closed question'. (Can be answered 'Yes' or 'No'.)

Whilst that may be true such a response is itself an example of the right answer to the wrong question. So I'll ask another question – the right question this time . . .

'What *happens that is different* between the reaction to the first question and the second?'

Answer: Each of the two questions sends the thinking on two completely different journeys.

In the first question – 'Do you know anyone that needs to talk about real estate today?' The immediate response by the brain is either 'Yes' or 'No'. If it is 'No' then the brain is immediately looking for a way to shut down the conversation and move on.

If it is 'Yes' we then hit the second barrier because the

94

question refers to 'need'. So if someone does come to mind, that person is then graded against the answerer's own internal definition of 'need'. Remember what we said in the opening chapter about communication – that everyone has a slightly different interpretation of every word. So for example my thinking or internal dialogue may answer 'well I know that Julie is looking to move house but that is 6 months to a year away, so it doesn't really constitute need.' And so my thinking will discount Julie based on my own definition of 'need'.

Whereas, of course the real estate agent would have loved to speak to Julie so that he could introduce himself. Then when she did do something later (ie move) she would think of him. The challenge is that the word 'need' is very subjective.

In the second question – 'Who do you know that needs to talk about real estate today?' The brain goes in a completely different direction because the fall-back on the mental reflexes of either 'yes' or 'no' are avoided. It asks, 'Who do I know?' 'Who do I know?' and immediately goes to the internal Rolodex. It is now searching the internal database and is mentally looking at names and faces of people that it recognises. The brain is no longer looking for ways to close down this small talk, it has actually been sent to a different place, a place where friends live! The answer no is not logical so the thinking has to *change*.

Both questions were aimed at eliciting the same result – to get leads. Yet one was far more successful than the other one. Such is the power of the right question.

If you want to improve your life start asking better questions.

The question is everything.

Let's recognise though that the important point here is whatever the thinking is, it is a response to your question. In effect, you are controlling the respondents thinking.

QUESTIONS ARE SOFTWARE

So if the question is everything, what is the question? Suppose you switch your computer on and you use Microsoft Windows. Microsoft is the interface between you and the hard drive, the machine, the memory. The quality of everything that you put onto that machine is, at the end of the day dependent on the quality of that software.

In the same way questions are the software for the brain. Questions are the software that exercises the extraordinary piece of hardware that lives between our ears. It *drives* our thinking.

Our mind has an enormous capacity for storing and retrieving knowledge. But that capacity is useless unless we can direct that capacity to create or carry out action. And it is the question that allows us to do that.

I had the following experiment relayed to me once, I thought it was clever so I tested it at a seminar I was conducting. There were about 60 people in the audience and I asked them 'Put your hand up if you remember whether there was a neighbourhood dog (as in four legged animal, not unattractive kid!) when you were growing up?'

About 50% of the audience put their hand up. I then asked, 'Do you remember the name of the neighbourhood dog? If you do, write it down.'

There was some scribbling in the audience.

I then asked this question – 'when was the last time somebody asked you that question?' and challenged those that responded positively; 'Put your hand up if it was more than 5 years ago, more than 10 years ago, etc'.

A 55-year-old in the audience reflected on the fact that it had been 40 years since somebody had asked that question.

40 years since that little piece of information was accessed. Wow!

That experiment illustrates a number of very powerful ideas to me. Firstly, the incredible capacity of the human mind to find information from within the memory banks. Even totally useless, irrelevant information. Secondly, that it would still be there at all after 40 years – where does all this information go? Can you imagine how much there is in there? Thirdly, the possibility that is implied by both ideas: How creative, intelligent and resourceful could you become if you could access all that you have ever discovered, learnt, seen, heard, spoken, thought and experienced – at will?

And finally the last powerful idea is the role of the question itself.

That little piece of information would have stayed buried in the recesses of the mind forever if the question had never been asked. Granted, the world was not made a better place by its retrieval. But the possibilities that its excavation demonstrates for us are enormous.

This is not about memory. It is about the application of the information that the memory retrieved. Memory isn't enough – we have to be able to bring the right pieces of information together at the right time. And questions allow us to do that.

We have to be able to retrieve all the memories relating to X so that we can formulate a conclusion from that pool of separate memories and the ideas they provoke – rather than just one memory of X. Only when we can pull together all the memories of X can we see the correlation between the information and the connections between cause and effect. We are then in a position to draw an informed conclusion about what to do for the best, rather than making a reactive choice based on one aspect or one view. Unfortunately most of our day-to-day decision making is only a question or two away from a better next step.

Our thinking has the habit of taking shortcuts through instinct, emotion and inferred meaning. If not trained otherwise this can lead to invalid conclusions about things and can influence our effectiveness. By being able to see the bigger and more complete picture you can circumvent the pitfalls of relying on those shortcuts and stick with fact and truth.

> How creative, intelligent and resourceful could you become if you could access all that you have ever discovered, learnt, seen, heard, spoken, thought and experienced – at will?

Questions are the tools for excavation. If the questions are right then you get the information. If the questions are wrong – you don't. Know this: once you know the nature of the outcome you are attempting to deliver, there is only one best set of questions.

But questions are not just about gaining clarity of thought. They have so many powerful benefits that are often overlooked because of their sheer simplicity. We are never taught just how powerful questioning is.

If you are lucky enough to have been exposed to sales training at any point in your life you may have been introduced to the power of questions. However even if that is the case so much of the sales training I have seen is more about man-euvering people into the conclusions that you wish them to arrive at. Rather than a process of integrity and honesty that arms people with information to make a considered judgment and draw a valid conclusion.

Consider: the right question can also put the questioner in control of the outcome and allows him or her to control the environment with much more skill. (This sounds like sales training and it may well be, but selling is managing thinking anyway.)

If you look at the process of negotiation the person who asks the questions is always in control. Whoever is asking the questions has the agenda. The great thing about this is that even if you are not the one asking the questions you can still use the Thinking System to pre-empt all the possible questions that you could be asked. So that you can enter any negotiation, meeting or discussion fully armed with the answers. And that is a very powerful position to hold whatever side of the fence you are on!

Good questions play a more important role in getting to the truth than good answers.

Questions can also be designed so that the answers are less prone to manipulation.

A simple approach is one we apply when we facilitate a workgroup through an assessment of their performance. At one point we need to get them to grade themselves. Our name for this process is 'True Colours'.

The idea of our 'True Colours' often scares workgroup leaders. They become concerned that their team will over-state the quality of their performance. In other words they will give themselves credit that they do not deserve. Let me tell you it *never* happens.

Quite the opposite. During the True Colours exercise the coach will invariably have to remind the workgroup that the benchmark for measuring performance is against their best potential outcome. Not against the best in the world or the best imaginable or even the best competitor. It's about how well do they perform measured against their *own* capacity to perform yet they still give themselves no extra marks. In fact they will typically tell us that they perform less than 15% of their processes to the best of the team's ability.

That same business owner, participating in the process with their team is now saying 'oh come on guys, we're pretty good at that, don't be so hard on yourselves!'

The trick is in the Question, which separates the individual from the process and de-personalises the entire benchmarking exercise.

If the Thinking System is sound – politics, back-stabbing and manipulation dies. Or better still, default settings are turned off, emotion is disconnected, a common language is distilled and the person asking the questions is divorced from the content! If someone wanted to manipulate the outcome, whatever their motivation, then they have to convince you of that outcome. And the only way they can do that is to manage the *information flow*. Where as a Thinking System allows the questioner to manage the information flow not the answerer.

And if you can't manage the information flow then you can't artificially influence the data to support your case. But if your case is sound, then it is based on fact, and will emerge in any event.

HOW TO ASK QUESTIONS – THE RIGHT WAY AND THE WRONG WAY

To ensure purity of thought and eliminate manipulation, the technique we apply is called Horizontal Sequential Questioning – the right way.

Simply this means all the answers to one question at a time, rather than all the questions for one issue at a time. The latter being Vertical Sequential Questioning – the wrong way.

An example of Vertical Sequential Questioning would be . . .

John:	(asking the workgroup): 'tell me a task that the company performs'.
Workgroup:	'manufacturing the widget.'
John:	'how well does the company manufacture that widget?'
Workgroup:	'pretty well'.
John:	'if the company were to manufacture perfect

widgets on-time, every-time – what would need to be different?' etc.

This is Vertical Sequential Questioning because we are asking one question and getting one answer. What happens if we continue this way and ask all the questions relating to 'task one' then all the same questions about task two, three, etc? Eventually people start to know what is coming and as soon as they know what is coming, they are in a position to be able to pollute the information to support their subjective points.

Horizontal Sequential Questioning for the same example would look like this.

John: 'tell me every single task that your company performs.'

Workgroup: they would then fire off all the tasks that the business does until that was complete and the workgroup exhausted the list.

John: 'tell me how well the company performs each one.'

Workgroup: would then go through the list and tell me.

John: 'tell me how each one should be performed.'

And so it would continue.

In other words we are first thinking *only* tasks, then the thinking turns only to performance. The workgroup doesn't know what is going to be asked next so they just answer the question – openly and honestly.

With Horizontal Sequential Questioning, if a person is trying to 'massage' the answer to question 10 they can't because they don't know the journey they are taking. They can't see or predict that question one – a simple and apparently innocuous question 'tell me every task' is going to be eventually followed by them having to say how well those tasks are done. They don't realise either that they are already authoring (say) their operational plan.

Also, when you observe things on a macro level, the problems on a micro scale dissolve. For example if you are heading into a meeting committed to making an issue out of something, and then see it lined up against all the issues the workgroup faces, you are overwhelmed by a sense of perspective and your thinking becomes clearer and more rational. In addition Horizontal sequential questioning often amplifies the 'groove' of thinking. When everyone is thinking about the same thing, the speed of thought increases and the momentum that is generated can move the workgroup ahead leaps and bounds.

Often someone has a part of their job that they don't enjoy and therefore don't do well, if at all. They may hope that no one notices (which, in our experience, can and does happen). With Vertical Sequential Questioning they could have either not told you about the task or lied about it. But with Horizontal Sequential Questioning by the time the workgroup gets to the stage of assessing the tasks they have already named *all* the tasks – there is therefore, no-where to hide!

Of course The Thinking System is not about trying to make people uncomfortable and 'catching them out'. It is about getting to the best thinking. And getting to the best thinking is all about asking the right question. The way we achieve this is by always separating the task from the individual. In this case the question was 'How well does **the company** perform that task' not 'How well do **you** perform that task.' By separating the task from the individual you ensure collaboration rather than potential for accusation. Even this one simple question took multiple iteration and application to confirm it was *the* right question!

QUESTIONS BUILD RAPPORT

Finally, questions also allow a person to *build rapport and develop relationships*. Something instructions don't always do

Here is another example of a Thinking System approach in the workplace that illustrates this point:

I once had a member of staff who was responsible for administration. A large part of her day was spent mail-merging letters and sending them out. I used to see her from my office. She would stand up and sit down maybe twenty times a day to retrieve something from the printer. The printer was only a short distance away but it was on her left hand side and she was right-handed, which meant that to retrieve the documents from her seat she would have had to twist beyond her reach to get them.

Being the systems freak that I am, it irritated me and I felt sure that it must also irritate her. But rather than going over to her and suggesting, or worse, telling her to move the printer – which was the 'obvious and logical' thing to do – I approached it differently. I wandered across to her as if I was just dropping by, made some small talk and then asked . . .

'What would you change about your workstation if you could?'

Of course I asked this question because I thought she would immediately mention the printer but she didn't. Instead she mentioned her chair and how she would change that. She mentioned a couple of other little things that we could also fix and then came the bombshell.

'You know what I particularly like is that the printer is on the wrong side for me. This means that I have to get up from my desk and get the material off the printer so I don't sit in my chair all day and get a sore back.'

This irritating distraction to me was a godsend to her. I learnt a valuable lesson about questions, subjectivity and objectivity that day. I took my perception of the situation into that conversation and it was the exact opposite of hers.

If I had marched over to her and said 'You know, this is really stupid, why don't you move the printer to the other side of your desk. Then you won't have to get up all the time'. I would have received any number of responses such as 'Well I would if those bastards in technical support would give me the cable extension I ordered 6 months ago' or 'Well actually I like it that way because it helps my back so it's not stupid to me'. Either way we are heading into a conversation most probably laced with hostility.

As a result this individual felt 'listened too' and that I cared enough to ask about her comfort in her workstation. We got to interact in a busy day and I got to see something from a different perspective. Instead of imposing my view on someone else, my view changed.

SO TO RECAP, QUESTIONS ALLOW US:
- To gain clarity of thought, which allows us to gather the necessary information and draw the correct and appropriate conclusions.

- To control the outcome with more skill and to control the environment around us – the one that asks the questions is always in charge.
- To illuminate the real issues and eliminate guesswork
- To open our thinking which allows the space for creativity to develop
- To build rapport and strengthen relationships and allow us to operate with honesty and integrity.

WORKSHOP

Imagine you overheard a member of staff being rude to a colleague. You don't want to make a scene but you want to make this person aware that he or she was rude.

Design a set of questions that would highlight to an employee that they had been rude to a colleague. The objective is to get that person to realise through questions that perhaps their conduct was not fair or necessary. But remember, the individual must draw the conclusion themselves rather than hear you pointing it out.

17

THE CASE FOR BUSINESS COACHING

It is not widely known that the word 'coach' comes from the Hungarian place name Kocs (pronounced kotch). Some couple of hundred years ago, in that town, someone invented a superior form of horse-driven state carriage. It became quickly accepted by the aristocracy not only in Hungary, where it was called 'kocsi' (meaning of, or from Kocs), but throughout Western Europe. The French changed 'kocsi' (pronounced kotchee) into 'coche', which then became anglicised as 'coach'.

Of course, the key component of this invention – indeed of any vehicle – is the wheel, which evolved from pre-historic times. At one stage a long-long time before the invention of the coach, the wheels used in Kocs were rather square-shaped. Riders complained a lot because of the bumpy ride so caused. According to local legend one enterprising coach-maker put a lot of effort into perfecting the squarish wheel. When he finally showed off his work to his peers the reaction was one of silence. Finally, one viewer managed to say: 'But it is triangular! What sort of an improvement is that?' The inventor heatedly responded: 'Of course it is triangular! Can't you see the benefit? One less bump!'

One day, all businesses will have a coach involved in their business, just as athletes are coached.

You realise of course that the local under sevens soccer team has a coach. And if seven-year-olds can take their soccer seriously enough to have a coach, then surely you can take your

105

business seriously enough to have a coach. It requires you to just come to terms with the fact that you don't 'think' as smart as you are, but with a coach you can.

I've talked to elite athletes and they've often said to me that the best coaches are not necessarily 'liked'. Because a good coach is somebody who's not afraid to ask you the *hard* questions. The good coach will mirror the athlete's real behaviour, the cold, hard reality of their behaviour and training patterns. They will not mince their words or cushion the blow nor will they sacrifice reality to make the task appear less daunting for their charge.

The fact that our thinking cannot be objective means that we need someone who is – the coach. The Thinking Limitations are no different to the biological limitations an athletics coach helps their charge overcome. Our thinking is simply incapable of being on both sides of an argument at the same time. Our thinking doesn't arrange itself to produce the outcome that reflects our best available conclusions.

Fact is you can't change people that much. What makes me *me* is very different from what makes you *you*. What works for me may not work for you so we have to accept that difference and embrace it rather than try to create clones. The words that help me understand ideas are the very words that might confuse you. The answer is in allowing people to author their own way. The last part of this book is dedicated to helping you do that.

The answer to business improvement does not lie in someone *else's* way of running a business . . . it lies instead in your ability to unpack and translate your *own* way!

> Don't waste time trying to put in what was left out. Try to draw out what was left in. That is hard enough.

In the international business bestseller – *First Break all the Rules* by Marcus Buckingham and Curt Coffman, this idea has been proven conclusively. The book is a product of two mammoth research studies undertaken by the Gallup Organization over the last twenty-five years. The study gave voice to over one million employees and eighty thousand managers.

What they found was that the greatest managers in the world *seem* to have little in common. They differ in sex, age, and race.

They employ vastly different styles and focus on different goals. Yet despite their differences, great managers share one common trait: They do not hesitate to break virtually every rule held sacred by conventional wisdom. They do not believe that, with enough training, a person can achieve anything he sets his mind to . . . People don't change that much. Don't waste time trying to put in what was left out. Try to draw out what was left in. That is hard enough.

CONTENT AND CONTEXT REVISITED

When we train people to be coaches we now train them on the theory, completely divorced from the discipline of coaching or the application of the theory. That comes later and independently. So first they learn the content, then they learn context.

Without conscious and persistent differentiation between content and context you are simply muddling through and lurching from one thought, idea or suggestion to another in the wild hope that something will stick! Sometimes it does but wouldn't you rather have consistent results? Think of the money, time and energy that you would save!

You see everything on the planet is divided into two categories.

◆ Things you *can* control
◆ Things you *can not* control

Which do you spend most of your energy on?

Most businesses spend *most* of their *thinking* time and energy on the things they don't control. Yet they preside over a huge number of underperforming elements over which they have total domain.

This is because we (people) cannot separate content and context when we are the 'subject'. This is why you ask others 'Why are you worrying about *that*?' and why 'others' ask you the same question.

If you are in total control of the things that you *can* control, you are in the best possible position to *influence* things that you *can't* control.

To do that, you need context. Without it you will often fail to even recognise the problem! But you don't have context. You can give it, but you can't have it. It's like a lap, you cannot sit in your own!

> **If you are in total control of the things that you *can* control, you are in the best possible position to *influence* things that you *can't* control.**

To get context, you need a third party. Today, anyone can call himself or herself a Business Coach (sadly) but in time, it will emerge as a specialist profession represented by people who know exactly what to ask you . . . and when!

I have found that everybody is as everybody is. (Wow that's profound!) So if you want them to be what they are not, you have two choices: you can *change* them, or you can *make it easy* for them. But I've already given you a clue as to the effectiveness of one of those options: it doesn't work. The fact is you can't change someone and even if you could why would you want to?

It's hard enough to find and nurture someone's natural talent without trying to ignore it and turn them into something else. Coaching allows everyone to see his or her own abilities more clearly. This leads to better placement of staff to specific roles which will lead to a happier and therefore more productive working environment.

That's why for a business to work properly and more efficiently, it needs to be coached. Everyone must be able to get clear about what they are here to do and release the rest of the noise that occupies their thoughts. Behind context there is complex theory, none of which is in this book, because to run a business properly you need the context not the theory behind it. A good coach will take control of the process, eliminating the need to understand the theory behind the process, instead simply ensuring that it happens.

So to the now well-tried division of labour: content is the challenge and responsibility of the workgroup and the context is the challenge and responsibility of the coach. Have you wasted your time then? No, because if you are the workgroup leader, then you need the context in these pages to get the most out of your team! It is *you* who need the Coach to get the same result for yourself.

Remember human nature is such that we'll make decisions emotively and then try to validate our decisions intellectually.

Because of this emotion we make subjective choices. We will buy the car of our dreams even though we can't afford it. We will still have a few too many glasses of wine tonight even though tomorrow we've got something important to do and we know we're going to have a hangover.

If you have a context into which you fold the content then emotion-driven decisions become less possible. Will you ever have a car salesman say to a teenager: 'Do you really need all that power?'

Don't kid yourself that your subjectivity is helping your business. Everything you're doing you're doing below your performance level, and the reason is that the software and hardware is fundamentally limited, and the only way to fix it is with objective facilitation – external management of the mind-trappers.

The personal development industry has its plethora of motivational speakers, all vying for your attention. It's no wonder that we are being hoodwinked into believing that we can reach our potential on our own. Oh, of course as long as we have that book, that tape and the overpriced conference!

In a sense the personal development movement has become the new religion. The enigmatic figures on stage

> **If you are the workgroup leader, then you need the context this book provides to get the most out of your *team*.**
>
> **It is *you* in turn who need the Coach to get the same result for yourself.**

engendering emotion reminiscent of a 60s revival meeting providing people with a 'formula for success', a 'formula for living' and an unreal expectation of our own potential.

Our experience is that, while you *do* have the answers to your own challenges, it takes these two discrete processes (Content and Context) to extract those answers. The missing piece of the puzzle is no secret to athletes who have long since realized the importance of an external force.

In order to get the most out of ourselves we need to be coached, coaxed and held accountable. Athletics coaches watch you run – you need someone to watch you think.

The fact is the business guru, motivational speaker or the high priced consultant doesn't have anywhere near all the answers – but you have most of them. What happens when the guru goes home or the seminar ends? Or when the consultant delivers the 80-page report (along with the sizable invoice)? Do you have improved skills to mine your own thinking and find your own answers? Do you have an increased ability to fire yourself up and take action?

And it's not that these 'gurus' have necessarily got it wrong. It's just that what worked for them may not work for you.

Not only that, many of these self-made 'legends' have absolutely no idea, consciously, what they did that led to their own success. And even if they do know, the chances of them also consciously knowing the specific steps required (never mind the syntax of those steps) *and* then being able to communicate that knowledge in a way that most would understand, is virtually impossible.

It's like baking a sponge cake. You could watch someone and take notes and even be given the recipe but that won't necessarily guarantee that you duplicate the result. The reason is that there is probably a little nuance that is unconscious – perhaps a dash of vanilla essence at the very end. The baker may not even be conscious of using it and so the magic ingredient is lost forever. You could have worked out 95% of the ingredients and technique but without that last 5%, which is unconscious, you will never recreate that cake.

Being able to unpack that additional 5% is the secret.

Your mind is like 1000 filing cabinets jammed full of information gathered over your lifetime. Chances are the 'system' for where everything went was based on where there was room left to stuff it! But over time your brain developed those default settings that give *you* access to that information in what appears to be a system. The problem is no one else has access. One day someone efficient starts in the office and decides to 'tidy' your filing cabinets. You are left in total chaos because they have messed with your system!

The truth is there is no system; there never was a system. Why? Because no one ever gave us one – at best you have managed to cultivate the skill of memory but memory training is about retrieval alone, not application, it does not constitute a system. Memory is nothing more than a container for information – not assessment and certainly not analysis. We must do much, much more than that. The Thinking System allows us to begin this process.

What the Thinking System does, particularly if applied by a coach, is it allows you to empty out the 1000 filing cabinets, get rid of the rubbish and subject yourself to a real methodology for accessing the valuable information left over. You suddenly go from 1000 filing cabinets to 100 and you save thousands of hours a year trying to find things that you 'knew were in the 64th cabinet, 2 drawers down in front of the Lammington file', the secret is that the 'system' translates itself into your language. It's interactivity (questions) ensured that you developed the protocols in *your* language and on *your* terms.

The process to get to that level of efficiency may take some time and commitment up-front but the long-term benefits for your business and sanity are phenomenal.

We have the potential for extraordinary clarity of thought, inspiring and ingenious creativity and inexhaustible ability if only we knew how. Our thinking is like electricity – an incredible power capable of good or not so good! Its use and existence is never in question however its application is varied and diverse. It is like having a power point behind the wardrobe. We have a vague recollection that it is there but we never bother to move the wardrobe to get access to it. The Thinking System allows you to plug into that potential and go a long way to overcoming these limitations on our thinking.

THE FIVE STAGES OF AN IDEA

The influence that a third unrelated party has on the development of an idea can be understood by unpacking the steps through which an idea passes as it moves from inspiration to commitment.

It is extraordinary how personal a process it is. Think in those terms as you read through them:

First, you get the idea . . . I will leave the neurologists to explain this phenomena but we know it as an 'ah ha' moment. Let's call this stage *Inspiration*.

111

Second, you convert the idea into an expression 'in your head'. Sometimes the idea cannot be expressed and it may die right there. Sometimes, having converted it into 'words' in your thinking, its shortcomings are exposed. Hence, in a team situation you get 'Hey, I know, why don't we . . . ah . . . no don't worry it won't work'. Let's call this stage (where the idea forms into thoughts that can be expressed) *Construction*.

Third, you express the idea. In other words it survives the internal construction and is ready for a public broadcast. So the idea is in the public domain now. Often it dies here. Someone challenges it 'But if we do that, how will we . . .' and you concede the point there and then. Often though, it passes this test. Let's call this third stage *Articulation*.

Fourth, someone repeats the idea so for the first time a stranger is looking after your 'baby'. Often, the idea dies here (I now wish I chose another analogy but let's stick with it) because it is *different* when the words are spoken by someone else, all of a sudden you *stumble* on some objectivity and it just changes complexion. Alternatively you hear it back and it sounds just as good as it did when you told yourself. Let's call this stage *Reflection*.

Fifth and finally, you or someone else writes the idea down. Sometimes the idea dies here, writing it down gives it a formality and perspective that is different and you discover its weaknesses. Alternatively it survives. Let's call this stage *Commitment*.

In our experience, ideas that make it to this point, to stage five, when emerging from a workgroup are likely to be 'good ideas'.

The Context in this situation becomes more important as you move through the process of thinking and assessment.

You can't ask yourself the questions you need to ask along the way because you are thinking of the idea not the questions! The scope for emotion to influence thinking at each of these points is self-evident.

I can go into a $1.5 billion business and ask half a dozen questions that change the way they do what they do. And I have not added any information. Nor have I necessarily suspected that what they are currently doing is wrong either.

I had a client that had a significant business. They had just

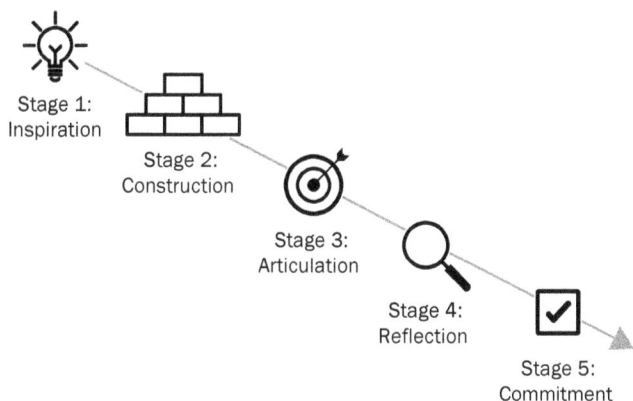

Figure 6: The Five Stages of an Idea – as easy as downhill for water . . .

acquired a subsidiary company. I asked them where that subsidiary company was located – it was in another capital city – I then asked them what their intentions were in terms of maintaining its location, and they said naturally that they would be retaining the Head Office in its existing location. The reason given for that choice was to minimize the disruption and impact on the new subsidiary.

I continued to question them about this with the aim of identifying whether any real thinking had been applied to the ramifications of that 'decision' – which of course was not really a decision but more an assumption based on the course of least resistance. So I asked questions like, 'What are the expectations of the subsidiary company about their likely location?' 'What might be the advantages or disadvantages of discussing and identifying the best location?'

By applying such a Thinking System to the situation a series of commitments were made which led to an opportunity for a significant part of the new subsidiary to actually change location and become part of the acquirer's business.

The people in that section of the subsidiary were happy because they saw a big advantage in terms of career opportunity by joining the bigger organisation. And my client was happy because it offered them some significant economies of scale that they had previously missed because content and context were mixed.

Using default settings, they had only taken their thinking far enough to confirm their suspicion that the Head Office didn't need to move. With the application of a Thinking System and the injection of some objectivity, (via the coach) they were able to decide what their ideal outcome would be and work back from that position to see if it was possible. What they found was that sure, there were parts of that Head Office that shouldn't be moved. But by examining the full extent of the decision and the full extent of the ramifications, they were able to achieve a middle ground.

Our problem is this . . . Looking at the facts above you are thinking, 'but that's so obvious!' Of course it is. Every one of the executives that I coached in this example would have drawn the same conclusion had they been outside rather than inside the problem . . . context.

I am living proof of the necessity for objectivity. I can go from one business and ask a set of questions that are important for them to come to the right conclusions about how they're doing something, and then the next day can be falling into exactly the same trap as my client.

Anyway that's my pitch for the coach. Ignore it or embrace it – it's up to you . . .

18

THE TWENTY MINUTE COURSE IN BECOMING A GENIUS
(The Complex Thinking System)

Psst . . . want to become a genius in twenty minutes?

Then you have come to the right place!

How would it be if you could know with some degree of confidence that if people came to you with a problem, you had an 80% chance of solving it for them! Now, if it were possible then they may indeed call you a genius!

It is possible.

The reason I can say this with absolute certainty is because everything has a source code. We have been hoodwinked into beleiving that life is complex. But the reality is quite the reverse. The expression of art is complex yet to the artist it's simple. Why? Because the artist has worked out the source code.

Take a moment to see if you recognise any of these songs or artists . . .

If I could turn back time (Cher)

Don't you love me anymore (Joe Cocker)

Don't wanna miss a thing (Theme from Armageddon; Aerosmith)

I'll be your shelter (Taylor Dayne)

Let's make it last all night (Jimmy Barnes)

Some classic hits and some major artists. You can almost imagine the moment of inspiration as they walked along the beach on sunset – infused by inspiration, tragedy, love or whatever, they rushed back to their studio to tap out this classic and create the masterpeice of music that the world recognises and applauds.

Mmm well actually No. All these songs were written or co-written by a songwriter called Diane Warren. A one-women music business! Quite obviously song writing is a system! I am not disputing her natural talent for it but there is a right way for writing a 'hit'. To the audience they are complex. I'm sure she composes them one note at a time . . .

What about sitcoms – we laugh at Seinfeld and think that it is such an original and unique idea. Is it really – look at the Mary Tyler Moore Show. A relatively normal one (Seinfeild and Mary) a headstrong woman (Elaine and Rhoda) a zany one (Kramer and Ted Baxter) and a quirky one (George and Murray)

Everything is a system – even DNA code is relatively short. All the genetic difference you see between people is actually contained in a miniscule percentage of the total DNA code.

It has to be this way otherwise the mutations would be too rapid and your first child might be a turtle!!

So taking this back to business and the short cut to genuis . . .

We have 'farmed' the contents of the thousands of business plans we have helped construct. Those plans dissect client companies right down to the most basic processes. We assess each process, set benchmarks, and then facilitate the action plan to close the gap between current performance and preferred performance.

We know that the team knows, even before we arrive, what the problems are. Our Thinking Systems (questions) help them to discover, in their own minds, the solutions. So, in short a database with an enormous amount of Business Problems *and* their solutions.

Now, what lies behind the failure to perform tasks to the level the team regard as appropriate is now clear to us. It is in the limitations on our thinking. These limitations manifest themselves in a number of ways. These ways used to be confused as being the problem, things like poor morale, lack of systems etc. These are only the 'symptoms'.

We examined these sub standard performances and

discovered that the limitations on our thinking leads to the manefestation of 10 recurring obstacles that inhibit performance. So basically the lack of good quality thinking will result in one of ten standard business challenges.

From a Coaching perspective this leads to a pretty simple formula. When a workgroup has a challenge, a simple set of questions tells me the problem. Then the right Thinking System allows the workgroup to solve it.

So how do you become a genius? In this context it is simple. I will share with you the ten 'obstacles'. They are simple and easy to remember. Then we will turn them into a Thinking System, meaning some questions that will help you discover which of the obstacles our friend with the problem needs to address. This will be our first 'complex' Thinking System, complex not because it is difficult, after all we are still just asking questions. Complex because it is one where you do *not* have a particular conclusion in mind. In that sense it is a 'pure' thinking system.

Going back to our statistics, we know that the workgroup has a solution to all the challenges they identify. We also know that they are right 80% of the time.

That means if you use this list of ten as your guide to the questions you ask, you will lead them to a solution for which, while entirely their own, they will feel compelled to give you credit! (Some credit any way!)

There are only ten ways poor thinking manifests itself in business.

Lack of a **System**:
A system is not a 'way of doing things' – that is a habit! A system is *the* way chosen from all the *known* alternatives.

Procedures not **Written Down**:
No use having a system if it is not committed somewhere in writing. It is a problem particularly when the person who typically performs a task is unavailable for some reason.

No **Accountability**:
If nobody owns the job then the shared blame will lead to poor execution.

No **Audit**:
It doesn't matter how important the task, if nobody is checking, then where is the motivation?

Recognition of **Importance**:
Often people are not fully aware (until some formal thinking process is applied) of just how important some tasks are. Small things can often have a domino effect through the business. When the team can see this, usually after they reverse engineer a process or two, they lift their game.

Lack of **Skill**:
Occasionally the workgroup does not possess or 'match' the skill to complete the task to the standard that they desire.

Lack of **Resources**:
Simply put, this refers to all the resourses excluding human skills and technology.

Lack of **Technology**:
The business may not have the Hardware or Software required to do the task

Change in **Structure**:
The person who used to do it well left the business or the business structure changed and the job was not re-assigned. This is an extraordinarily common problem in small business.

The Benchmark is **New**:
It may be that the team has only just latched onto the idea for improvement.

There you go. The Ten Obstacles workgroups place in the path of their potential. Simple but powerful. Our experience indicates that they can solve their problems 80% of the time. They just have to recognise it. Let's bring together all that we've discovered. We need to turn these obstacles into questions and we need to use those questions as a catalyst to bring out the information needed, thus allowing the person or team with the problem to solve it for themselves. So let's make a template based on these ten manifestations (including a brief definition).

<u>System</u> (a way of doing/addressing the tasks selected from known alternatives)
<u>Written</u> (the system committed to paper or electronically stored, accessible to all)
<u>Accountability</u> (one person in the workgroup who knows implicitly that they are responsible for the desired outcome and the process)
<u>Audit</u> (a way of checking that the process is followed or the job done the way it should be)
<u>Importance</u> (a clear understanding of the impact the process has on the rest of the business)
<u>Skill</u> (the capability or knowledge required to perform the tasks to the identified standard)
<u>Resources</u> (the tools, equipment, capital and facilities needed to do the tasks properly)
<u>Technology</u> (the software and hardware)
<u>Organisation</u> (the structure to support the person accountable – e.g. to provide that person with specialist skills)
<u>New</u> (assessment of the time needed to bring the new idea to life)

Table 1: Template or checklist for developing Thinking Systems

Imagine now that someone has come to you with a Business challenge. How do you respond using the template?

For start, you could turn each of the ten items into a diagnostic question that will begin the journey toward the solution.

But let's be creative about this and avoid questions like 'Do you have a System?' Go for something like 'Tell me about the system you have for that'. Both questions presume that a System is needed but one allows them more scope. The answer to the first question could be no. The same person answering the second question may say, 'Well, we *sort* of have a system' Then you can ask 'What do you mean by "sort of"?' and that will get you closer.

Now it is over to you. You have the ten factors that took ten years and a few million dollars to distill. All you need to do is this: Memorise the ten underlined words and jot down some questions that will help you work through the list to help your friends and colleagues find the solution to their problem.

System (a way of doing/addressing the tasks selected from known alternatives)
Do you have a System?

Written (the system committed to paper or electronically stored, accessible to all)
Is it written down somewhere?

Accountability (one person in the workgroup who knows implicitly that they are responsible for the desired outcome and the process)
Is someone accountable?

Audit (a way of checking that the process is followed the way it should be)
Do you check?

Importance (a clear understanding of the impact the process has on the rest of the business)
Do they know how important it is?

Skill (the capability or knowledge required to perform the tasks to the identified standard)
Have they got the skills?

Resources (the tools, equipment, capital and facilities needed to do the tasks properly)
Do you have the resources?

Technology (the hardware and software needed)
Have you got the technology?

Organisation (the structure to support the person accountable – e.g. to provide that person with specialist skills)
Has there been an organisational change?

New (assessment of the time needed to bring the new idea to life)
Is it a new idea?

Table 2: A No-brainer Thinking System

When you apply this Thinking System you work down the list. So if their answer to 'Tell me about the system you have for this' was compelling and they obviously *did* have a system, you would default to the next obstacle (Written) with a question like 'So where are these pearls of wisdom written down?' Again if their answer was compelling you move to (accountable) 'And if I visited your team and asked the person responsible for the job to put their hand up, would someone enthusiastically and immediately raise their hand?'

Using this technique you can coach your team to their own solutions. In the case of your team, you may already know which of the ten applies and you can begin your questions proximate to the answer.

When you ask a question they cannot satisfactorily answer, get ready to hear the prophetic words 'You know, I think that's our problem . . . we don't . . .'

We are now ready to put the thinking behind us and start the Application . . .

System (a way of doing/addressing the tasks selected from known alternatives)
Tell me about your system for tackling this. (assumes they have one)

Written (the system committed to paper or electronically stored, accessible to all) **Where would this information be typically kept? (assumes they document it)**

Accountability (one person in the workgroup who knows implicitly that they are responsible for the desired outcome and the process)
Who would regard this as being their job? (assumes assignment)

Audit (a way of checking that the process is followed the way it should be)
How do you know that it's not being done properly? (as 'challenge' implies)

Importance (a clear understanding of the impact the process has on the rest of the business)
Has the impact of this task on the rest of the business been explained?

Skill (the capability or knowledge required to perform the tasks to the identified standard)
What is the typical skill set you need to get the job done?

Resources (the tools, equipment, capital and facilities needed to do the tasks properly) **What could you acquire in terms of resources to make it easier to do the job properly?**

Technology (the hardware and software needed)
Tell me about the software that drives this process?

Organisation (the structure to support the person accountable – e.g. to provide that person with specialist skills)
How long have you had the problem?

New (assessment of the time needed to bring the new ideas to life)
How long have you been trying to accomplish this?

Table 3: An Empowering Thinking System

You now have a toolkit to diagnose problems. If the team does not volunteer the problem, simply start with – 'who is happy with the way we . . .?' They will probably answer that they are not. You then 'default' to the above Thinking System.

EXERCISE

Devise a set of questions, your own Thinking System, using the chart below.

System
Written
Accountability
Audit
Importance
Skill
Resources
Technology
Organisation
New

Part Four:

PERFECT THINKING – PERFECT BUSINESS

Our tendency to under perform is mostly an expression of the limitations in our thinking.

These limitations stop us from creating a mode of operation where our performance matches our knowledge.

In the past we have written this off to be evidence of poor attitude, lack of opportunity, lack of encouragement and other symptoms that have launched a million books.

In reality what they unwittingly perpetuate are typical workplace characteristics like lack of systems, failure to record knowledge, failure to provide accountability and the others explored in Chapter 18.

To improve business performance we need to get people to behave in ways that address the real problems and thereby overcome the limitations. And to do that without expecting them to change their personality, in a way that works *with* rather than *against* the way they, as adults behave and learn.

In Part 4 we look at the characteristics that workgroups inadvertently develop into behaviour that successfully combats these limtations. By understanding such behaviour – that *accidently* compensates for the limitations – we can distill the techniques behind them, recognise the Thinking Systems they represent. Leaders can then apply them in their own environments.

Understand the characteristic, apply the related questions and it should start to come to life for you.

19

GETTING STARTED

There is a thought experiment, known as the Chinese Room, which was devised by the philosopher J Searle(*). His purpose was to illustrate the difference between behaviour and understanding; to show the pitfalls in trying to assess one's capability (knowledge) by watching one's behaviour (the symptom of knowledge) alone.

Imagine the task of translating between Chinese and English performed by an operator sitting in a closed room with an appropriate rulebook. It is quite possible to supply him/her with English text as input and have Chinese text returned as output provided the rulebook is extensive enough. The operator need not know any Chinese to appear to the observer to be a linguist!

Similarly, the computer known as 'Deep Blue', could be seen as having a powerful intellect as evidenced by the behaviour of winning at chess.

Lesson: You do not need to have knowledge in order to exhibit behaviour.

Awareness is the first step toward every solution. Armed with the awareness and understanding of the problems and their solutions we can begin to look for application of the solutions.

Remember the statistics that we discussed earlier. Workgroups always know that they perform only 15% of their tasks well. Note also that this is the same whether the response comes from a good company, a bad company or a just plain ugly company!

> **On closer inspection we realise that the good companies do certain things almost instinctively that the bad companies just don't do.**

This doesn't change the fact that the performance of good and bad businesses, relative to each other, is very different. On closer inspection we realise that the good companies do certain things almost 'instinctively' that the bad companies just don't do.

Typically, whatever this behaviour is, it is unconscious. Another characteristic we note is that they appear to be evidence of the unconscious application of the Thinking System. If you remember back to the Chapters on Thinking Systems, and the concept of 'talking backwards', you probably recognised it as behaviour you have seen exhibited by someone you know. My guess is that if that is the case it is likely to be someone successful. It is likely the behaviour was one that the person you have in mind engaged in 'naturally'.

These behaviours are what Part 4 is dedicated to. They will be presented for you to easily emulate so that you don't have to go through years of trial and error to develop them. They will be readily applicable and will help you convert your business into a powerhouse, by *behaving* in a way that overcomes for your *team* the limitations that we have uncovered in Part Two.

I have called these behaviours and the Thinking Systems that go with them *New Realities*. What's 'new' about them? The context! Since we have a biological impediment to our ability to make changes to the way we approach solutions, any solution we look at is 'new'. Rather than pretend to be the first to recognise these behaviours and their importance, which I am not, I am re-stating them as outcomes, that are only possible to achieve when we have compensated for our thinking limitations.

They are 'realities' because we cannot deny their value towards success. Particularly if quality of life and workplace experience play a role in your assessment of what success is. The 'reality' is in that you either build a workplace that reflects these characteristics or you accept the performance gap. You cannot 'realise' the latter without embracing the former.

So, these Seven New Realities address effective workplace behaviours expressed in a new context.

The theory of why they work is there for those who want it. But be assured, the Thinking Systems we explore will work regardless of your understanding of the theory! Remember, the people who behave this way, do it unconsciously.

The Thinking System makes it possible to adopt the innate characteristics evident in successful businesses without understanding the psychology behind them or needing to know how they work in a scientific sense.

The techniques promoted here also allow us to encourage the behaviours by others that are facilitated by the New Realities. We will see this demonstrated later. The challenge is to provide your workgroup with a framework that allows them to feel empowered, inspired, productive, valuable and needed. This not only creates a more effective and efficient workgroup but also a more harmonious and enjoyable one too. And all of these things ultimately affect your bottom line.

The New Realities are cumulative: each one assisting the next. Applied separately they are very powerful facilitators for change. Applied cumulatively they are exponentially so. This cumulative benefit creates what we call a virtuous circle . . .

VICIOUS CIRCLES VERSUS VIRTUOUS CIRCLES

Everyone knows what a vicious circle is. Most of us have experienced one at some time in our lives. A vicious circle is a downward spiral, where one bad thing leads to another to another and you can't get out of the self-reinforcing negative loop.

For example, two candidates are going for the same job, one is unemployed, and the other is currently employed. They both have exactly the same skills, same knowledge and same experience.

Yet if you ask employers whom they would employ based on that knowledge alone – the typical answer is 'the one who is employed'.

So the person without a job has just missed out on the very thing he or she needs (and the person who's got the job has just got the very thing they *don't* need – although they may *want* it – they don't need two jobs). That's a vicious circle for the one who missed out.

The lesser-used flip side to the vicious circle is the virtuous circle. In fact most people don't even know that virtuous circles exist. Why? Because virtuous circles are either not consciously recognized or they are put down to chance.

The critical difference is that vicious circles are often apparent and the virtuous circles are often not. In addition the reason one is understood and recognized and the other is not is that *people will often trace their bad luck but they don't consciously trace their good luck.*

Successful people don't generally know why they are successful – they put it down to various platitudes but in the end they are *thinking* smarter. Because you don't watch yourself think, how could you know that – it is innate, it is accidental. No context – no learning. You can have success without learning! If I repeat what works it may work *again*. But . . . I have not *learnt*. Successful people don't watch themselves think – get it?

They can't tell you because they weren't *there*. They only participated in content (their effective behaviour) NOT context (watching themselves behave). Till someone one day points out to them, in third person language, what was so effective in their behaviour and why, then they get their very own 'ah hah' moment. You need both content and context to learn. It's not that successful people don't *want* to tell you – they often *cannot* tell you.

This book is in itself an imposition of *context* on what has always been *content* for me! It has forced me to *explain* what was historically instinct to me.

So . . . now I have *unpacked* that instinct, Part 4 will show you the blueprint for thinking that can be *replicated* through *simple behaviour* and make your outcomes successful even if you (in isolation) shouldn't be!

You see when something goes wrong, people tend to be more introspective and analyze or at least look at their behaviour. This may not even be a conscious process but the fact is that the question 'why did this happen to me?' will almost automatically pop up. The power of questions will ensure the analysis because if you ask one, your mind is forced to answer.

On the other hand when something goes right we have a

tendency just to be happy about it and celebrate. Therefore contemplation usually doesn't occur. Yet this is exactly the answer to the puzzle: What is different between successful people and unsuccessful people? Successful people have an innate desire to trace their good luck as well as their bad. Because instinctively they know if they trace the effect back to the cause they will be able repeat the behaviour that brought them 'good luck' and avoid the behaviour that brought them 'bad luck'.

You've heard the saying 'The harder I work the luckier I get'. In commerce, luck is overrated. It is usually just a case of uncovering the patterns and behaviours that when re-applied over and over again in the form of hard work will yield the positive results.

Luck is what happens when opportunity meets preparation. Successful people are simply repeating positive behaviour protocols that they've built for themselves or had all along.

The need is therefore twofold – the process of introspection that we do when things don't go well is just one step in the process. We then have to ensure that we learn from the experience and do not go on repeating the same error in different disguises. The challenge with a virtuous circle is this: we not only have to accept that it happens but we have to consciously engage in introspection so that we can find the common denominators to our success and transfer them into other areas of our life. For the most part, in the pages that follow, I have done this for you! The Seven New Realities on their own can hardwire the 'luck' into your business and your relationships.

Take for example a business owner who is known for being a listener. Ask such individuals why they choose to listen to their staff. In most cases the response would be one of surprise at the question. You see, people who do this naturally, assume that everyone does it and therefore the question seems pointless to them.

A typical response might be 'of course I listen to my staff'. Now let's unpack what is actually happening in the organisation as a result of that demonstrated behaviour?

The two obvious things are that a) the listeners may end up

with ideas they didn't have before and that b) the relationship between them and their staff is improved as a result.

The not so obvious things are the little cultural nuances that can gather their own momentum and create a positive impact in the business. Staff can see the interaction where one of their colleagues has said something to the boss and has actually been *listened* to. As a result their perception of the business changes. The person then draws the conclusion that they are part of an organisation that listens. This makes people feel valued and that their opinion does count for something and this has a positive effect on the whole environment.

Others in the organisation see that the company has listened and consequently they themselves are more likely to come forward with their own ideas. Let's say that the ideas that come forward, or the ideas that follow, are good, and lead to savings, either greater revenue or less expense. Now there is more money to spend on more ideas that are coming more often from people who are more motivated to share ideas within an environment that they enjoy.

Voila . . . a virtuous circle.

Yet most business owners would not say to you 'well there are a number of discreet reasons why I listen to my staff. First, it means everybody realizes I listen, this means I get more ideas from my staff and some of those ideas turn out to be good so I implement them and then more ideas come from more people more often and so my business is more profitable'. The answer instead, typically is 'well, doesn't everybody?'

The reality is that not everyone does. Instead, they exhibit a very different symptom. That symptom comes from thinking 'well if I listen to the staff then they'll take up all my time, then everybody will want my time to give me their "stupid" ideas, and besides we don't have the budget to do different things and it works just fine as it is'.

During my experiences which comes from unpacking and rebuilding (or analyzing and synthesizing if you prefer) so many businesses I have discovered that these virtuous circles are in effect the results of good behaviour. These are now crystallized as the New Realities.

Each of the New Realities is derived from the behaviors

exhibited by effective workgroups. And, again, they inadvertently address the four limitations discussed under the headings: Default Settings, Emotion, Communication and Context.

Bringing your business into line with the New Realities means starting to demonstrate behaviours, which individually, are in and of themselves positive and profitable, but when put together create a virtuous circle. Each one makes the other possible, in different degrees and to different extents; most importantly each one is ultimately an expression of good thinking and becomes imposed context, or the automatic way of thinking. Each one is a Thinking System expressed as a behaviour.

BEHAVIOUR VS KNOWLEDGE

As I pointed out before, it's amazing that often when we meet people who are exceptionally good at something, we find that they are the last to draw that conclusion. They tend to think that if they are good at something then everyone else must be too. Alas, for you and I, this is not the case.

The vital point, however, is that you do not need to understand the 'why' that makes such a person exceptional, you just need to understand the 'how'. The 'how' is the Thinking System that allows you to duplicate the behaviour without understanding the social science behind it and still get the results.

Often it's actually behaving that way that teaches you why it works, which is again the way adults learn. If they do something that turns out to have a good outcome they go 'oh, that worked, I might do that again'. That is if they are *surprised* that the outcome was good.

They forget that three months ago at a barbecue at their brother's home, who is also in business, or their sisters, who is also a professional, someone said; 'You should try this'. Once they tried it – probably by accident – and found that it works, it becomes part of their automated behaviour – so long as they recognize the connection between the outcome and the action.

You see with kids, they know they don't know and have no ego attached to that fact so they get an idea by being given some suggested action, they go and try it and if it works they transfer that idea into knowledge. It's almost like an internal checklist where kids try some suggested thing, it either works or it doesn't and they then incorporate the resulting information as knowledge.

Adults on the other hand stop doing that as soon as ego shows up which for most of us is somewhere in our teens! Suddenly we stop trying things on suggestion and so our knowledge stagnates. For us to learn we have to do the behaviour, witness the outcome, connect the two and then come up with the idea ourselves! This then forms a natural loop of learning and negates Myth No. 1 in Chapter 1 (if you get only one idea from this conference . . .).

It's more a bit like the 'fake it till you make it' philosophy! Now I am not suggesting that you do that necessarily but what I am suggesting is that if you incorporate the behaviours outlined in the next seven chapters and don't get too hung up about the why's then you will see results. How fast you then reverse engineer that knowledge into a virtuous circle is your own personal evolution.

Remember at all times . . . these are behaviours which compensate for the Four Limitations. The Limitations are permanent, biological facts that cannot be self corrected. Therefore the need for these 'Realities' is universal and their application compulsory.

Let me explain the layout of the Chapters to signal their value to you.

There are six components:

1. Title.

The title introduces the principle for each New Reality. It is important because in time they become hooks between your behaviour and a level of conscious competence in the application of Thinking Systems. You will start to think and see Design = Motivation (the first of the new realities) in your work and your interactions. Don't dismiss the chapter headings as catchy hooks, however tempting it may be . Commit them to memory instead.

2. Precis.

This thought starter begins to scope the reality and explain its connection to performance. This is the language you might use if you wanted to explain the New Reality to, say, a team member.

3. Behaviour.

This is a brief description of the behaviour that might indicate the presence of the right 'thinking', which is in turn a catalyst for the right behaviour. Remember that it is behaviour some of us have developed as a kind of unconscious attempt to overcome the Four Limitations. Not everybody does it, but successful people do, and successful workgroups exhibit the behaviour.

4. The Rationale.

A detailed look at what makes the behaviour work in our favour and, especially, how to apply it most easily. Where appropriate specific reference is made back to the limitations on our thinking.

5. Workshop Exercises.

These are designed to help you to begin to shape your behaviour and ultimately your thinking. They are simple and straightforward. You only add the questions, which become to a degree self evident in the exercise itself.

6. 'Reality' Check.

This closing thought links the New Realities together demonstrating how they become 'Virtuous Circles'.

20

DESIGN EQUALS MOTIVATION

'People are never stronger than when they have thought up their own arguments for believing what they believe. They stand on their own two feet that way'

~ Kurt Vonnegut – *Hocus Pocus*

PRECIS:

People are naturally motivated when given the opportunity to design their own plan for success and put that plan into action. When they do, it's no longer work: they're doing something for which they can see a purpose. In other words, put the meaning back into the job and it's not a job; it's a personal mission.

Think about some work project that truly motivates you. It's not always that you enjoy the process: it's more often that you like the outcome because you see value in it. Workers at all levels respond the same way.

THE BEHAVIOUR:

We have consistently found in good businesses that decision making and inventiveness flow as easily from bottom up as they do from top down. The behaviour we look for is a strong meeting discipline. This means that opportunities are hard wired into the business to allow people to 'have their say'. As a consequence people will begin to program themselves to have things to say, so in turn they take a mental note of issues that might improve the business performance. There is often a strong performance management discipline in these businesses as well. That way people know that the time will come when they can comment on the performance of the business as well as their own performance.

THE RATIONALE:

The first of the New Realities is *Design Equals Motivation*. Quite simply people are motivated by the opportunity to design their own success and there is no greater motivation than to feel you are the engineer of your own future. In businesses that get the most out of their potential, there is evidence of a culture of inclusiveness and contribution to design throughout the team.

Remember the question in the Introduction: 'Will you ever get 100%' from your people? I said no. But I also said you should be able to get to 80% or 90%. A 25% improvement. Why?

Normally, if you ask your staff to do more work, they will expect to be remunerated for that change in their job description. But if you change the culture or the ethos of the company to empower employees to highlight shortcomings and allow them to find their own solutions, they will become more productive and more fulfilled. Remuneration might never be an issue. More importantly, if your staff begin performing to a higher level of efficiency then the business should be booming and so there will be more to share around!

One of the characteristics of effective workplaces is the evidence of an environment where people are encouraged to have control and influence over the way their job is done. This requires effective workgroup leadership behaviour. Good leadership is where the leader fosters a feeling of control by the workgroup and assists people to find within themselves the answers to their own questions. Thus allowing their people to come up with their own ideas which triggers the required motivation. Equally, the effective leader allows the workgroup to come up with the leader's ideas. There are books on this subject but they are complicated and concentrate on theory.

With the end in mind, let's talk about the sort of environment that a good leader is striving to produce, because replicating that is simple. Again, you don't need to understand the science behind the behaviour in order to replicate the behaviour. You just need to understand the symptoms. The first symptom is, letting people have control of the way they do their job. Let them come up with the ideas that are needed for the business to improve.

This New Reality is clearly vital and the Thinking System most aggressively addresses *this need*. The key in this new reality is first getting 'others' to discover. Then supporting this approach with opportunities for the team to participate in design. That means design of all aspects that impact on the job they do. It doesn't mean abrogating responsibility or delegating your authority away. It means three things:

1. Talking Backwards
2. Behaving like a genius
3. Creating opportunities to invent.

TALKING BACKWARDS

You now know how to do this. You want something done for a reason. Give the reason before the something. It is easy. Wear an elastic band around your wrist or a piece of sticky tape over your finger or something to remind you for a week or two to remember. And don't take the idea to its extreme just to make a liar out of me!

The approach is best used when what you are about to ask:

- Should be done by someone else, not you,
- Requires a new approach,
- Will take someone out of his or her comfort zone,
- Your gut tells you they might be put out by the request, or
- You are hesitating in any way before asking.

In these circumstances you need to 'talk backwards'.

This can be done through the application of a simple Thinking System as described in Part 3, Chapter 15.

BEHAVING LIKE A GENIUS

Apply the approach discussed in Chapter 18. Stop giving answers to questions and start asking the questions outlined in the 'formula for genius'.

If a staff member has a challenge and you have a solution, at the very least take your suggestion and turn it into a question.

Simply put: instead of 'Why don't you . . .' becomes 'Would it make sense to . . .?'.

Can you see that if your colleague has any issue with the suggestion, if you expressed it the first way . . .' Why don't you . . .' you are likely to get a dishonest response. But if you express your suggestion the second way a healthy discussion will ensue. In other words if you tell me 'do this' and you are wrong *and* you are my 'boss' my thinking goes 'how do I disagree without hurting the relationship?' and that is not a productive train of thought. This mental response is almost completely avoided if the suggestion is couched in the second way. The brain defaults to the answer to 'Would it make sense' with 'yes but' or 'no because'.

You have the role of the Coach in this instance, and if there is one thing a Coach never does it is give an instruction. Really great Coaches don't even make suggestions! You rarely win if you do. Even if you are right then you have hurt the respondent. (Hey, don't argue with me on this point, just accept it!) Ultimately it *perpetuates* the approach and desire to get the solution from someone rather than from themselves.

If you have an idea for an approach to a challenge, then it has to be *based* on something. Those 'somethings' are all answers to questions. Those questions are easy to distil. Ask them and reverse the process – talk backwards. In time they ask themselves and stop needing you! Believe it, it works.

If you ask some questions and they find the answer, you have lost nothing. They may assume you knew all along – so what? But they will have shared ownership and that equals motivation.

CREATE OPPORTUNITIES TO INVENT

Just convene a meeting to discuss the business with the team.

Some Thinking Systems to apply:

'How do you think we are going?'

'What do you all think we do best?'

'What's the least effective practice in this business?'

'What's the most effective practice in this business?'

'Round the room quickly, what's the one thing about this company you would change (apart from me!)?'

'What are our competitors doing that we are not?'

'What's our point of difference?'

'Who's our best customer? What makes them the best?'

'Pick one other person in the room, if you were them, what would you change? And why?'

'What is one initiative we committed to but failed to deliver on, and how can we fix it?'

'Have I forgotten to follow through on any promises?'

'If we were going to hire someone tomorrow, what skills would we bring in and to which department?'

Each of these questions is designed to uncover a well-known and predictable problem. As an exercise, look at each question and jot down what issues you think would or should surface.

THE ROLE OF THE WORKGROUP LEADER IN *DESIGN EQUALS MOTIVATION*

Invariably effective workgroups are found where the workgroup leader is able to communicate in the language of each individual, a characteristic of effective communicators.

I remember reading an article about Bill Parcells. Parcells is nothing short of a living legend in the world of American Football. His team-management career has been punctuated by moments where he took incredibly under-performing teams and turned them into champions – and he has done this on a number of occasions without the revolutionary change in playing talent that you would anticipate. In his article in the Harvard Business Law Journal he put this down to the fact that he manages 'collectively individually' (my words not his, but I think they sum it up). The cornerstone of his management is coaching and the cornerstone of his coaching is one-on-one communication, just as the cornerstone of effective leadership has to be one-on-one communication.

What does that imply? It implies managing the team by managing the individuals within the team first, then the team as a unit evolves. The understanding here is that if everyone in the team knows what is required of them and what to expect, then the team will function by default: effective coaching strategy.

So the cornerstone of effective management style is *coaching* – one-on-one communication – and,

The cornerstones of communication are the *questions* you ask.

The action that the business owner can take here is to re-read Chapter 15 on the Thinking System and start to develop questions that can lead to these design and discovery outcomes. Remember, the secret is to ask questions that are aimed at getting the other person's mind to collect the pieces of information needed, to draw the conclusion that you're after.

CONCLUSIONS VERSUS DECISIONS

'How will I know I'm on the right track?' Simple, you will feel it and that feeling will emerge from conclusion based rather than decision based management.

Knowing whether you have made a decision or drawn a conclusion lies in your degree of comfort *after* you've made the call. When you draw a *conclusion* there is practically no discomfort. Why? Because the basis for drawing a conclusion is to know and feel that you have all the evidence you need – you've got all the facts.

Most *decisions* on the other hand are to a greater extent part fact and part assumption and part guess and part hope!

Conclusion: I have all the facts
Judgement: I have all the facts I can reasonably secure
Decision: I do not have all the facts

Leaders are forced to make decisions when they know they've got all the information that they either can get or that makes commercial sense to get. They have the experience to assume the rest. So leaders are in charge of that delicate balance between how long to wait before making a decision and how much information to gather and rely on. The further down the chain of command you get, the more you find the need to be drawing conclusions.

It's a conundrum, because the further up the ladder you get, the more sophisticated the thinking, the better placed you are to draw conclusions.

Now ... I'm not telling you when to make a decision or when to draw a conclusion. I'm simply pointing out the difference. And if you understand the difference you understand the Thinking System that little bit better because the Thinking System is the question generator, or 'source code' for extracting the facts – faster. And the more questions you ask, the more facts you get and the more facts you get the greater the chance of being able to be drawing a conclusion rather than making a decision ... Simple!

Design Equals Motivation is about using questions to help people collect the information necessary for them to draw conclusions – often the same conclusion that you might have started with. It is about asking the right questions so that you empower them to find their own answers, their own ideas and therefore feel motivated and inspired to achieve success by means of taking action toward achieving their own self-designed outcomes.

THINKING SYSTEMS AND MANIPULATION

You may at this point be thinking, 'Hold on John, isn't that manipulation?' Well, it isn't. The difference is that manipulation is feeding twisted information so that it causes someone to come up with a polluted conclusion. Manipulation can also be achieved by limiting the information by only asking the questions that will uncover the information that will force you to make the decision I want you to make.

For example in our earlier story of the disappearance of Augustine Le Prince in Chapter 11, I could have read only half the story and left you feeling very uneasy about Thomas Edison. That would be manipulation because I would have deliberately distorted the facts by limiting the information in order to get you to feel angry toward Thomas Edison. Manipulation is about engaging emotion to direct a person to a particular 'selfish' conclusion. And this example has already shown you just how easy it is to do that. Imagine how much of what we read or see in the news every morning is tainted by the emotion or the motives of the correspondent. It is the easiest thing in the world to play on someone's emotion and therefore control someone's conclusion. (Remember, emotions cannot distinguish between fact and fantasy.) That's why professional speakers do it. It bloody well works every time and it's bloody easy!

Note that language plays an important role too. When I was working my way through University I had a job as an Oil Industry Consumer Sales Manager. I was actually a console operator (bowser attendant) in a petrol station but that description simply did not pull the chicks!

Using Thinking Systems on the other hand takes courage and commitment because you are creating the framework for the truth to emerge – good, bad or ugly. It takes courage to uncover the truth and be able to look at it objectively and clearly without getting worried about what it means about you or your company's performance. But awareness is the first step to cure so whilst it requires some initial courage to pursue the truth in case it turns up bad news, the long-term benefits far outweigh any short-term discomfort.

The Thinking System is about asking questions that will allow a person to access all of the information necessary for them to draw the right conclusion for them.

For example it is easy to tell someone to do something. The four limitations propel us this way. It takes thought, courage and trust to replace an instruction with a question. Because you can't control what conclusion the person will draw from the question. You have to be open to the possibility that they may know more about this particular task than you do, in which case you will either need to be prepared to ask another question or have enough faith in your people to let them run with their own conclusions.

WORKSHOP EXERCISE:

Technique 1 – Simple Thinking Systems
Design a Thinking System.

Select an outcome you want to encourage your team towards.

In the boxes marked F1 through F5 think of five facts or reasons that drive the outcome – that make it relevant and worthwhile.

Then construct a question, to which the answer could be that fact or reason.

Record the experience below, after you try it on the team.

	F1	F2	F3	F4	F5
Facts					
	Q1	Q2	Q3	Q4	Q5
Questions					

Figure 7: Developing purposeful questions

Technique 2 – Re-Engineering
As we mentioned earlier the best way to teach adults is to have them do something and then look at the results. So in order for your business or workgroup to adopt these protocols they must be encouraged to do it as a matter of course.

The best way to introduce *Design Equals Motivation* into the team is by introducing a new aspect to your weekly meetings. Each week assign a workgroup member the task of preparing a presentation to the group on a process that they are responsible for: why they do that process, why is it important for the business and why is it done that particular way. That person is to share the prepared material with the workgroup at the next meeting.

As the facilitator of this process it is very important that you separate the individual from the process. So encourage the individual to say 'The company performs X task', rather than

'I perform X task'. This way you remove the personal attachment between the individual and the process and allow a more impartial and open discussion in the group.

The last stage of the exercise is to open the process up for discussion and brainstorm different ways of doing the process. Remember when you brainstorm: first, write everything down – however stupid it seems to start with – then look at the answers as a group, consolidate and distil them.

The other members of the workgroup add objectivity to the process because they often don't know that much about it. However for this to be a valuable activity the owner of the process must draw the conclusions as to how best to change the process. That individual is motivated if she gets to re-engineer the process not if everyone else tells her how to re-engineer it.

At the end of each meeting congratulate the participants, especially the person who owns the process under scrutiny. That person is then asked to go away and re-design the process the best way she sees fit and report back to the group at the next meeting. At each meeting a new person is assigned to present until everyone has re-engineered at least one of their core processes. You can continue with this exercise until all processes have been done or move on to a different workshop.

21

KNOW EVERY OTHER PLAYER'S POSITION

PRECIS:
The second New Reality is this: Teams combine better when their members have a clear knowledge of other members' job definitions. In other words, if I am teaming up with you, your job specification is my business too! I need to know if you're a Front Row Forward, Ruckman, or Goalie. I only know how I can relate to my workgroup members – or for that matter, whether I should bother – when I understand how their jobs help me do mine. And how much they rely on me to do theirs.

People who see meaning in their job also want to be relied upon, being needed is great for the ego short term . . . and great for the career long term!

THE BEHAVIOUR:
Successful businesses appear to have a higher level of 'collective consciousness'. The people in them seem more acutely aware of what their colleagues do than is the case for businesses that struggle. They have sophisticated Induction and Orientation procedures, they have procedures that are written and communicated. They have an organisation chart. They let staff 'talk' to each other. They have a social calendar.

THE RATIONALE:
One of the things that we have found while unpacking businesses and observing patterns of what works and what

doesn't, is that many of the accepted paradigms of business are in fact flawed. One of these paradigms is about this New Reality called *Know Every Other Player's Position.*

If we ask ourselves the question 'Is it good for everyone within a workgroup to know what everyone else within the workgroup does?' the answer is invariably yes. The logic is quite overwhelming that this would be the case. However if we ask specifically *how much* people should know, the answer (the paradigm) always is that superficial knowledge ought to be sufficient. The concern it would seem is that too much knowledge will over-burden them because too much information can be confusing and distract them from their own specific role.

Our experience though tells us that the opposite is true.

What we've discovered is that this idea of limiting the knowledge sharing is totally flawed. We have yet to find the point at which too much information adversely affected a person's performance or productivity.

Instead, what we've discovered is that provision of more information has extraordinary value for the business. When I first began Coaching I found there was some resistance by people participating in my workshops. They felt they were being involved in analysing parts of the business that they weren't necessarily involved in or contributing to. And this meant it could occasionally get – dare I say it – boring.

Later we discovered (by pushing on with the process) that whether or not people were going to become bored when dealing with an 'unrelated' part of the business was dependent on how the situation was handled by the coach. If those persons were encouraged to see the value of their objective viewpoint on the process, they suddenly became 'facilitators' along with the coach, because they were truly separate or isolated from that process, their point of view mattered. We took them from zero *content* to being part of the *context.*

Typically in a business, if you are not the doer of a job, you are a beneficiary of that job being done, or you rely on that job being done in some way, shape or form so that you can do your job effectively.

One of my observations of performance is that you can't be a part-time anything if you want to be perfect in it. That is you can't do anything in life perfectly or to your potential unless it's all you do. If you spend every day doing what you're doing, you'll get better at what you're doing, and eventually you'll be the best you can be. I still believe that to be a valid observation.

So why could I expect that when I was taking people into parts of the business that they weren't related to, that they would actually be getting better at the part of the business that they were involved in? Wasn't I causing a distraction from their full-time job?

Firstly, I wasn't asking them to do it, I was asking them to understand it as we unpacked it, so the distraction was not permanent, it was temporary. That being made clear to them immediately took the pressure off people and they became interested and curious rather than skeptical and suspicious. When their interest was so raised they became more productive and helpful with answers or possible solutions and so they started to see the big picture more clearly.

Which leads me to the second insight . . .

Imagine you give some kids 50 Lego pieces. They are restricted in what they can build simply by virtue of the fact that they only have 50 Lego pieces. They can only build a certain number of things. Correct?

But suppose you give them 950 more Lego pieces to make a total of 1000 Lego pieces. Can they build more things? Yes they can, of course they can. Now here's the killer – if you then take the 950 away and leave them with the 50 they started with – what do you think happens?

Logic would say that they would then be restricted to what they could build before when they had 50 pieces. But the fact is that they can build different things, because that experience with the additional pieces created a better perspective about what's possible with the *original* fifty pieces.

And the same thing, I concluded, happens in a business. If you understand where your Lego pieces fit into the big picture you can become much more creative in your area and also within the business as a whole. So it's absolutely vital that you know every other player's position because it will always impact, even if only marginally on what you do and how you do it.

It's important to acknowledge that a symptom of effective workgroups is a broad understanding by all people in all parts of the business, and that there is a transparency in the performance of all parts of the business.

Try to imagine for a minute that people actually do care about how their performance and their job impact others. Then you start to see an environment emerge where people say, 'hey, I've got an idea about this thing that you guys do. I thought that if I change this then you could do it that way and that would be better for you. Would that help?'

Or when somebody's unavailable to fulfil a task, you don't then have a complete ignoramus who says 'well, you know I'm sorry, there's no-one here at the moment who looks after that'. Now the person can have an intelligent conversation with a customer and the customer feels as if the whole business knows them or the whole business is smart. It conveys an impression to customers that it's an effective workplace they are dealing with.

The 'net' is that what you want to accomplish is worth having your team members understand – collectively and individually. It makes for better team members. What we've also discovered out of this insight is that this inclusive approach is giving workshop participants effectively an M.B.A. in their own company, and that's a real bonus for them and the stakeholders.

Colleagues often experience a real paradigm shift when we work through this process. Every time we do an Operational Plan with a workgroup – every time – at some point, and often at many points, somebody will turn to someone else and say 'Geez, I didn't realise how much you had to do'. Once the rest of the team watch as the coach unpacks what each individual does, they realise what that person faces every day, the difficulties and challenges and the processes and procedures. The journey brings the workgroup together often with renewed respect and understanding and they become a force to be reckoned with!

Knowing Every Other Player's Position is about understanding the impact that you have on the people in the organisation, and the expectations you have of them.

WORKSHOP EXERCISES:

Technique 3 – Virtuous Circle

The workshop for this new reality is actually a by-product of the workshop for *Design Equals Motivation*. By choosing a process and then sharing with the group the details of that process, the rest of the group by default becomes aware of that player's position. They may previously have known that she did a certain process but hearing why she does it that way and what impact it has on the business opens up understanding – not only of her role in the company but also the business itself.

Technique 4 – The business 'Spin the Bottle'

Tell everyone in the workgroup to think of their Key Performance Indicators (KPIs) and ask them to identify the one most important one for each of them. Every week, perhaps after the usual agenda of the weekly meeting, ask a pre-elected workgroup member to challenge another member of the team with the following statement.

'I need you to do__ *(insert name of task)_*, so that I can __*(insert name of deliverable)_*, and deliver against _(insert KPI)____ key performance indicator (KPI).'

For example Louise says to Joanne: 'Joanne, I need you to give me the sales figures for the week by no later that 12.00 on Fridays, so that I can complete the sales analysis report and deliver against my KPI, which is to provide the sales report to Karen by 4.30 every Friday.'

The first 'blank' in this sentence (sales figures) will often not be a KPI for the person being asked the question. Therefore they are not very motivated to complete that section of their job. But when it is made clear to them how that affects this other person and her ability to meet her KPI then they can bargain with each other.

Providing the sales figures to Louise is not one of Joanne's KPIs so she does it if she's not doing something else and it's usually the first thing to get missed if something unexpected comes up. She might have just thought Karen was being difficult when she hassled her for them every week at 12.30. Now that Joanne understands the consequences of her actions on Louise she is more likely to provide what Louise needs when she needs it.

What happens in this situation is that they can start to bargain and come to an understanding. For example in this case Louise could say 'well I know you are really busy on Fridays so would it help if you didn't have to give me the stock level report until Monday morning and instead concentrate on the sales figures on Friday.' This compromise, which only came about because of sharing of information has not only allowed Louise to meet her KPIs but also improves communication and rapport between two employees.

Why not add, 'KPI re-engineering' to your regular weekly agenda.

'REALITY' CHECK

As mentioned before, at the conclusion of each New Reality we will reflect on how they have a cumulative effect.

Design Equals Motivation means people perform better when they're given an opportunity to design their own way to success. *Know Every Other Players Position* is about understanding what everybody else in the company does. Understanding what everybody else in the company does makes you a better designer, so by helping people understand what everyone in the company does, and then empowering them to design their own solutions, you now have somebody who's likely to design solutions that are closer to the workgroups' needs. This is why you've got this *virtuous circle* like improvement all the time in such a business: 'I design a way to do something, I find out more about what you do, I get a chance to re-design, and each time I increase my potential.' And remember that *the journey towards potential will always improve it.*

22

HIDDEN DUPLICATION

PRECIS:

The third new reality of business: The real problem is not that people don't do their jobs. It's that they do jobs confusingly similar to someone else's.

This 'hidden overlap' produces costly duplication. 'Hidden overlaps' happen because two jobs or two processes may be totally different in themselves. But if the benefit to the organization from their 'set of outputs' is the same, then it's overlap in terms of outcome and one of the tasks or processes is unnecessary.

THE BEHAVIOUR:

Simplicity of tasks and processes is achieved not through any deeply scientific analysis but through 'unpacking' the tasks ordered against their purpose, rather than their content. All the behaviours for 'Know every other players position' apply here. The business is likely to require cross-functional teams to review procedures. Key Performance Indicators are clearly articulated and as a result people think backward from the outcome rather than forward through the processes they control. This way they 'find' ways to shortcut the process.

THE RATIONALE:

Hidden Duplication is not people doing the same thing. It's people doing two different things for the same end result or reason. *Hidden Duplication* usually is a problem in business because people work from the beginning of their tasks to the end instead of from the end backwards.

To get the best results when trying to work out what to do – start with the desired result or outcome and work backwards from that.

This is actually simple logic but is done surprisingly rarely. Part 2 of this Book explained why. How often are we asked to do something and without the faintest idea of what it is, never mind the detail, we agree and go off on our merry way. Bumbling along until we get to the result we think we were looking for. Wouldn't it be easier if we just stopped for a second and asked, 'where is it we are trying to go', 'what is it we are trying to achieve'. Or . . . (thinking about some of the more universal outcomes like customer satisfaction) . . . 'what is everything we do that is supposed to deliver this outcome?' It doesn't happen largely because it's a context question, not a content question.

Remember the example earlier when I asked Karen to do an audio program for me (Chapter 9). Apart from highlighting the challenges we face in communicating with each other it was also an example of the need to be really clear about the end result and work back from that point.

So rather than blindly walking off into the sunset and hoping for the best, when we applied some thinking to the situation (some context) she came up with the questions necessary to start to build a path *from* the objective. Without that thinking it's virtually impossible to arrive at your destination in the shortest, most efficient time possible. The absence of thinking is the home of trial and error management! And hey, it's where most people live!

To avoid *Hidden Duplication* you must know what your outcome is first and work backward from it because then you will be more efficient and you will uncover the duplicate operations within the business. For example, let's say there are two departments in a company. One contacts clients for service (information A) and the other for relationship building (information B). Why are they ringing the customer? What's the underlying motivation? The underlying motivation is customer satisfaction. But the nature of the calls, the subjects, are two different things.

When given a chance to reverse engineer each other's procedures, the two jobs are discovered. The result is the realisation that the outcomes of quality service and relationship building are both very important. The business is then in a position to draw the conclusion that although they are different tasks the outcome is the same and so two jobs could have become one. That *Hidden Duplication* can be eliminated and once it is, one job can be properly allocated to one individual who becomes accountable for regular, consistent and monitored client relationships.

An obvious example for the above would be obtaining sales figures that would also be the same figures that the customer retention and loyalty department might require.

Hidden Duplication happens because people tend not to work back from the outcome. Instead they move forward through tasks until they get to the outcome, or they describe the <u>task</u> instead of the outcome they want:

Say I needed to send a package. Somebody says to me, send this to Karen. And I go 'okay, what's her address?' I then phone a courier. And in the process of phoning the courier I think, 'oh hang on a second, how urgent is this?' And I probably only decide that when the courier company says, 'VIP or standard?' That's working from the front to the end instead of from the end backwards. Working from the end backwards is to define the outcome, and defining the outcome is defining the whole of the outcome, right?

So the job is to get this to Karen, but the outcome is 'Karen needs to be in possession of this by 8 am tomorrow'. Now that I've described the outcome, I can work backwards from it. Does anyone live near Karen that might pass her place on the way home? Yeah, you do – great. I've just met the outcome AND saved the courier fee, because I've worked from the end backwards.

But this is not a habit, dear reader, it is a science and it is impossible without context. You as workgroup leader can supply that context.

This New Reality is the one that's going to test most people, because if you don't have the courage to really try to get inside this thinking, then you'll just convince yourself that it's not an issue and it can go on undetected for years.

Nobody wants to duplicate if they can avoid it. But to be able to prevent it you need to have the tools to unpack your business focusing from the end backwards. And that tool is you. (Your friends were right – you are a tool!) You need to be prepared to put all your processes under scrutiny, and you need to be prepared for unexpected outcomes, because if it's hidden you can't know beforehand what it is. To do that you need to bring your workgroup together and put those processes under the spotlight.

Hidden Duplication can be found by looking at the core processes and *defining* the expected outcomes. Then *working backwards* and looking at how the business actually delivers those things, and in that context the workgroup then start to discover things that are *overlapping*. Suddenly the discussion opens up and you start hearing things like, 'hang on, if you're doing that to get that, why don't I just do this when I do that, so that you won't have to do that any more'. Or 'if you need this to get that, why don't I make sure you get that by then?'

Sounds easy and it is. Important . . . Yes. Is this a shameless plug for coaching? No. Businesses don't exist for an infinite number of reasons, the key motivators are defined by the 10 or so Core Functions. Surely each is worth one brainstorming session a year?

I would love to be more specific about *Hidden Duplication* but the nature of the beast is that it is hidden! Therefore there is only one way to find it and that is to actively look for it.

WORKSHOP EXERCISE:

Technique 5 – Reverse Engineering Outcomes

Pick an important outcome in your business – say Client Satisfaction. With the rest of the workgroup list every process or procedure that must happen in order for your clients to be happy with your company. With each process look at who does that process and how it is done currently. Look at when it is done in relation to the other processes and is there anywhere else it could be done in the sequence and could someone else do it. Look for places where different tasks can be done simultaneously that currently are done in a conveyer belt fashion.

Your mission is to remove one person from that process.

By doing this exercise you can identify more readily when a process is getting slowed down. It is important to remind the group that this is not about individual people, it is about the process and, again, this workshop is an open forum for discussion and bargaining between the members.

During this process you can facilitate a 'Job Auction'. For everyone that is removed from a process and for everyone that subsequently does a little bit more – swap different parts of the job.

For example, Gillian and Wendy realize through this exercise that it would be much quicker if Gillian did the whole process rather than half of it and pass it to Wendy. Then they can look at what other processes they may share and Gillian could then off-load one of hers to Wendy in exchange. It can be a fun exercise and also a great insight for you as a manager because you get to see what processes (if any) people love and hate.

There is sometimes a tendency in all of us that if we hate doing something we assume that everyone else does too. But the fact is that your idea of hell could be someone else's idea of heaven. If you apply the techniques for these new realities in the way set out at the end of each chapter you will allow the workgroup to understand these differences so that everyone can do more of what they like and less of what they don't and still get the job done!

Of course it would be unrealistic to think that you can only do what you like and that there will always be someone who likes what you don't. But if you do these workshops at least you are in a position to identify any compatibility gap if it exists. It will lead to more harmonious and efficient workgroups.

Occasionally when you unpack a process to this level you may find that there is nothing else that you can do to make it better. But what you will much more often find is that there are glaring inefficiencies brought on by the passage of time and a 'we have always done it that way' mindset.

'REALITY' CHECK

Hidden Duplication is about making sure that you're not doing two different things in order to achieve the same outcome. Surely the chances of finding *Hidden Duplication* rely on our opportunity to understand and *Know Every Other Player's Position*. If I know what the other people in the company do, I'm more likely to find *Hidden Duplication*, and if I find that *Hidden Duplication* and you empower me to be the designer of my own solution, then I will re-design it to improve it and avoid *Hidden Duplication*.

23

IN TIME RIGHT BECOMES WRONG

PRECIS:

The Fourth New Reality states that the right solution becomes the wrong solution in time. If being different in the marketplace is really a marketing advantage – and it is – then you can't create and sustain that advantage by trying to hold onto a stock strategy. If anything, the context is changing so rapidly today, any business initiative that suited a marketplace more than a few years ago is almost certainly obsolete!

You may be very attached to a strategy or tactic, like you value your CD collection. But songs are based on sentimental attachment: commercial realities are far more brutal. If your competition finds a better way to do something, your old strategy will cost you market share; no matter how appropriate it was in its time. You can be as good as you were last year, even slightly better, and actually be going backwards!

THE BEHAVIOUR:

We have found that good businesses have a level of anticipation that sets them apart from their peers: they seem to leave old ways behind before those become redundant. Procedure manuals get updated regularly in these workgroups. Customers are surveyed to provide valuable feedback on service relevance as much as quality. New staff are invited to be objective and speak their mind about how they perceive things are done, competitors are observed as a matter of course.

THE RATIONALE:

If you go to the supermarket, to the perishable goods section, one of the wonderful things that you find stamped on all the goods there is the use-by date. This miraculous little invention makes sure that when you take the milk carton home, and pour it on your cornflakes, all the milk doesn't slide out in one big cube!

It's one of the most useful advances of the 21st century – particularly for the unsophisticated shopper!

The little known fact is that every process in your business has its own inherent use-by-date. In its current form it only has a certain shelf life. This is another one of those 'scary thoughts', and it basically sends a message to any staff member that whatever it is they're doing, however comfortable they might be doing it, it's only effective temporarily.

Now, I'm not suggesting that every process changes every day! What I am saying is that every process is on its way to becoming redundant and therefore every process, depending on its purpose, reaches a point when it is appropriate to sit back unpack and repack it again. In many cases it might be repacked very similarly to the way it was, the change might be minimal. Therefore the better businesses, the better workgroups, are the workgroups that are constantly challenging their own processes and procedures.

Business is a very fluid, alive and changeable entity. It is constantly changing whether you like it or not. So go with the evolution and watch the business morph into something else, metamorphosis is the new permanent state for thriving businesses.

LIVING WITH CHANGE

Let me suggest a new definition of 'change': Change is what happens when everything stays the same two days in a row – that's change. Status quo – the normality for business – is that tomorrow everything will be different. Therefore it becomes important to find the things that can be systematized so that they can be self-adaptive to changing requirements – wherever possible.

This is a cultural thing and the workgroup leader's

responsibility and obligation is to create an environment where things are questioned. That can feel at times like 'working without a net'. The challenge is the fact that we have never been given the tools and understanding to be able to face that challenge in a rational and logical manner. If you are given the challenge without the tools to deal with it then of course you get nervous. Remember the first time you drove? It wasn't exactly something that you just jumped in and did – there was an element of adrenaline.

And being able to change a process is a skill in itself that needs fostering.

Understand that *In Time Right Becomes Wrong*. What you need to do is have a planning discipline that challenges every core process and sets a date for reconstructing that process on a rotational basis. So unpack everything you do, look at each one and say, 'Are we doing this as well as we can?' If the answer is yes, ask the question, 'When's the next time we should look at this?' In any event, don't leave it longer than a year.

It may be that when you revisit the process there is nothing better that can be done to improve it, in which case move on. But what this diarised reassessment does is make sure that your processes are current and applicable TODAY. It can also highlight where shortcuts have been made or evolved that are not conducive to the end result. It creates an opportunity to audit the process. (Remember – you should be doing this backwards!)

In most instances we discover that processes are redundant *well after* they've become redundant. The mindset that you're after is this: healthy questioning, or healthy doubt about the system. Quality workgroups are workgroups where people do challenge the entrenched aspects and procedures of the business. The danger is confusing questioning with change.

Questions illuminate the need as well as the pathway for change.

This whole process can help take advantage of the new skills and objectivity that recent additions to the team might bring. Instead of teaching new staff the 'way we have always done it' we can use the new arrivals' fresh eyes as a way to reassess the processes, add new perspective – you may then get to see something that could make the process faster or more efficient.

What you are looking for is to program the mind to be questioning the process. But that's hard, it means changing people, so *you* need to do it, provide the context that is. It's more important than trying to make the process perfect. I'd rather have somebody who's asking about the process and challenging the process than somebody who only exerts their energy making the existing way of doing the process perfect. When somebody's getting a result, and has a healthy suspicion about the process, then they will avoid the problem of having processes questioned only after they've failed. In most businesses, the time at which we question the way we do things is when we find evidence that there needs to be a better way – they have already poured the sour milk on the cornflakes!

When people question, the worst outcome possible is knowledge, and knowledge is not a bad outcome for any business process. *Because if you question it, it does not mean it changes, it just means its chance of being wrong is reduced.*

Unfortunately processes in business don't carry easy to see warnings and sometimes they don't even have outward signs of dysfunction. Don't wait till your staff and customers get a mouthful of lumpy milk before you act. Instead be aware of when the process is likely to go 'off' and be proactive.

It may not be that it is not working anymore but there may still be a better way. But don't sacrifice commercial reality and profitability for dictionary definition 'perfect'.

While you may be thinking that this makes sense, let's not forget that what we've created is a fundamentally sophisticated way of thinking. One which most people have never learnt and do not engage naturally. True, it may be difficult to implement and the only way they can unpack what they do and question it is in some formal context where they're given an opportunity and assistance (yes, by you!). A business ought to be looking at all of its core processes on a regular basis and giving people some time out to question them, creating both a capacity and opportunity for the team to do so.

And a final point: remember the Staff Value Equation mentioned in the introduction where the illustration I had was of staff who used only 60% of their capacity. For 100% pay.

When I shared this with an audience once, somebody piped up and said, 'well, that's actually a load of crap, because I've worked out what the capacity of my staff is and I pay them what they're worth'. The more I thought about this proposition, which seemed at face value to have some validity to it, the more ridiculous it became to me.

What this individual was saying was, 'I'm prepared to accept the deficiency, I have assessed what my staff 'do' today and put a price on that activity.' Yet what he has actually done is pigeonhole his employees' performance and remuneration. Does this mean that if he does help his staff improve their efficiency, there will immediately be a contingent liability to pay them more as well?

He is drawing a rigid relationship between remuneration and effectiveness. Whilst people do want to be paid what they're worth, an individual's desire to do well is not entirely a matter of being financially compensated for it. In the businesses that we have worked with the need is far more often about the individual wanting to be told they are doing a good job as well as wanting to be effective.

We have to look at the opportunity differently and accept that people make an effort to and get compensated based on market forces for their work. Therefore if they only bring 60% of their potential to that work and we don't lead them to improve, then it is not right, it is not fair for them or for the business.

WORKSHOP EXERCISES:

Technique 6 – Innovation reporting

With the workgroup, identify the 10 most enduring processes in the business. These will be the processes that have stayed the same for the longest time without change. As a group try and force yourself to come up with a different way of doing it. Be as outrageous as you like because often it is in a seemingly ridiculous idea where there is a kernel of possibility that could revolutionize the business. Make it into a game.

You could give points for the ideas. You could offer a prize for the best idea – voted on by the team of course. You could have a debate, one side defends the current way, the other argues for change.

Technique 7 – Innovation culture

Put a value on innovation and set a target. Make it known throughout the organisation that innovation is rewarded in some way. It could be that the staff member responsible gets a bonus. For example, someone in a process may highlight a way for the same outcome to be achieved but with less expense – that person may get a percentage of the savings. Or standardise it and implement an innovation bonus scheme.

Talk-up innovation. If someone does a good thing or comes up with a moneymaking or money-saving idea, make it your top topic of conversation for the week. Tell everyone – 'Have you heard what Karen did?'

'REALITY' CHECK

In Time Right Becomes Wrong recognises that eventually the processes and systems in the business will become out of date. Well surely, if I *Know Every Other Player's Position*, I'm more motivated to identify where the potential weaknesses in the processes are. If I'm allowed to and encouraged to be the *designer* of my own methodology or my own process, I'm more likely to be looking for those parts of my job or those parts of my processes and procedures that are likely to become redundant. I'm more likely to look at them because:

(a) You gave me the opportunity,
(b) Because I now see it as my responsibility and
(c) I will enjoy my job more – and be rewarded for it.

I'm empowered – I know that I'm allowed to – and therefore I'm more inclined to. In many cases people don't re-engineer because they don't think that it's their role or that they've got the authority to re-engineer.

24

EVERYBODY HAS A RIGHT TO KNOW THE SCORE

PRECIS:

New Reality number five. Knowing you are making progress makes the job more satisfying. Every concentrated thinking exercise always establishes a clear destination . . . a destination that everyone involved thinks is worthwhile. It must always include a system for letting them know what progress is being made towards the destination.

You have a right to be travelling home at the end of every day saying to yourself 'that was worth every minute'. Or reaching the end of the week and saying 'that was worth every day'.

THE BEHAVIOUR:

Strong businesses have strong reporting disciplines. The difference is in the connection between the reporting and the performance of the *individual*, which typically is more comprehensive and focussed than the reporting of the performance of the *business*. Appraisal disciplines are in place, supported by a succession plan. If the business is too small for any formal succession then the workgroup leader is sponsoring Professional and Personal Development Programs for their staff. The performance of Staff is measured and reported against. There is a link between those reports and the performance of the business. The workgroup Leader walks past people and says things like 'Great job on the ABC Pitch Mary' and 'We got that shipment out thanks to you Dave'.

THE RATIONALE:

This New Reality is about keeping people aware of the impact that *they* have on the business.

There are two schools of thought around for such disclosure. First is the mushroom approach that basically specifies that you keep your employees in the dark and feed them bull. No one admits to adhering to that school but I am constantly amazed at how many do behave as if they did!

The second school of thought is equally untrue. The idea that your team will be motivated by the opposite is also misguided thinking. Imagine charts and graphs all around the office that cry out about the company's philosophical approach, and the company's targets, and where the company is at in relation to those targets. The current view is that this approach motivates the workgroup. More bull.

Generally it doesn't. At least if it does, it is pure coincidence and only works for certain types of people. The fact is nobody really cares about how a company is going. Well maybe they do – but if they do – it's only to the extent they see a direct connection between *their own contribution* and the way the company is going. And if you want to see this reality in action then concentrate on highlighting how each individual specifically impacts on the business success.

There's no doubt that the effective workgroup leaders are those leaders who are able to develop relationships that allow them to very quickly get into the minds of their employees and understand what motivates them.

This is why sales teams are so motivated by their performance, because it is typically measured by sales, which is *their* KPI, but their outcomes are erroneously construed as the company's KPI's. The manufacturing crew are rarely as excitable because no one has taken the time to make a direct connection for them between what they do and the overall performance of the company. Only when people see a connection between those things are they really motivated by them.

For example, in our business we run workshops, and they involve – in case of a small business – a company being 'locked up' for a couple of days off site. We have in the past employed a 'Workshop Co-ordinator' whose job it is to book the venues.

Part of that is selection of venues and making sure venues we use understand our requirements. Because of the depth of material we cover in the time that we spend with the client, essentially this off site venue is our office! It's an extension of our company. This means that the client's experience in a conference centre or hotel at which we conduct our sessions can have a dramatic effect on their view or perspective about the quality of the outcome and therefore . . . us.

I was talking to our Workshop Co-ordinator one day and she was explaining some of the challenges that she had with venues. The conversation got to a point where it became appropriate to make it clear just how important it was to be really tough on venues and make sure that they performed.

So I asked her if she was aware of the way our 'Extraordinary Guarantee' worked. (In our contract with our clients we have this Extraordinary Guarantee. If at the end of the workshop they are not completely satisfied that we can deliver against our promise, a number of things happen. One is that we then pay the venue costs and issue a full refund to the client. In addition we pay the clients' staff who turned up to the workshop at their published hourly rates for the two days they spent with us!)

Clearly, if the venue fails to perform, then that could contribute to a client's dissatisfaction and lead to a claim on the Extraordinary Guarantee.

That makes the Workshop Co-ordinator the *custodian* of the Extraordinary Guarantee, and ties what is an apparent procedural job into a very specific and direct outcomes-related job. Letting her know the score is about tying her performance to the claims ratio against our Extraordinary Guarantee.

So knowing the score means keeping the scorecard very close to the individual. Knowing the score is about personally attaching or helping people understand the impact their role has on the outcomes of the organization. That then becomes their incentive to perform. It also defines accountability.

Now you could be thinking, for example; 'that sounds fine John but I've told so-and-so a hundred times that we need to have that part in the warehouse by no later than the 15th of every month yet they never get it right.'

The key to ensuring that everyone knows the score, like with all of the New Realities and, indeed with all of this book, is getting us as leaders to move away from 'telling' and toward 'asking'. Because if you ask the right questions and therefore engage the right thinking, the person will realise why it is so important to have the part at the warehouse by no later than the 15th of the month.

You don't tell people their importance by telling them how the company's going, remember a person can perform miserably and the company can still go well, and a person can perform exceptionally and the company can still perform poorly. And people are motivated most by some sort of measurement or benchmark about their own performance.

Now, what does that mean in terms of workgroup performance? Effective workgroups are managed by very clear and identifiable Key Performance Indicators (KPIs) that are measurable and measured regularly, because that delivers a heightened sense of accountability and competition against themselves.

It can never be a negative for an individual to know and to receive the most *specific* feedback. People thrive on feedback yet, what we typically find is that there is no performance appraisal process. There is no regular appraisal of staff, there are no written job descriptions, and very often it is because the business owner regards these as an *imposition* on their team.

Each time we find those circumstances, we discover that through the application of a Thinking System (see Fig 8), we can bring to the attention of the business owner the fact that without exception, staff want job design or job descriptions, and staff want appraisals. People want to know where they stand. Business owners that interact a lot with their staff might think that because they spend so much time with them they are really 'appraising them all the time'. That is simply not true. And it's also a very unproductive way to manage people by sidestepping the formality of measurement and appraisal. Working with someone is sharing content, appraising someone is applying context. Workgroup leaders can and need to do both.

Appraisal is a necessary and desired part of business life. How else can we grow and learn and become better? There is a

The Facts are the 'Inspiration' for the Questions

QUESTIONS

| Do you keep track of your Business Performance? | Why is regular review of the Financials important to you? | Is it likely your team share this need to know what they are accomplishing? | What systems do you have in place to make it happen? | So are they striving to achieve goals they invent or goals that matter to the bottom line? | What's your strategy for improving your outcomes then? |

FACTS

| Knowing how you are performing is important. | It's the scorecard that tells you it's worthwhile. | The motivation is universal. | Telling people occasionally that they are good is not enough. | Targets and goals make people perform better. | Formal and structured reviews need to be considered. |

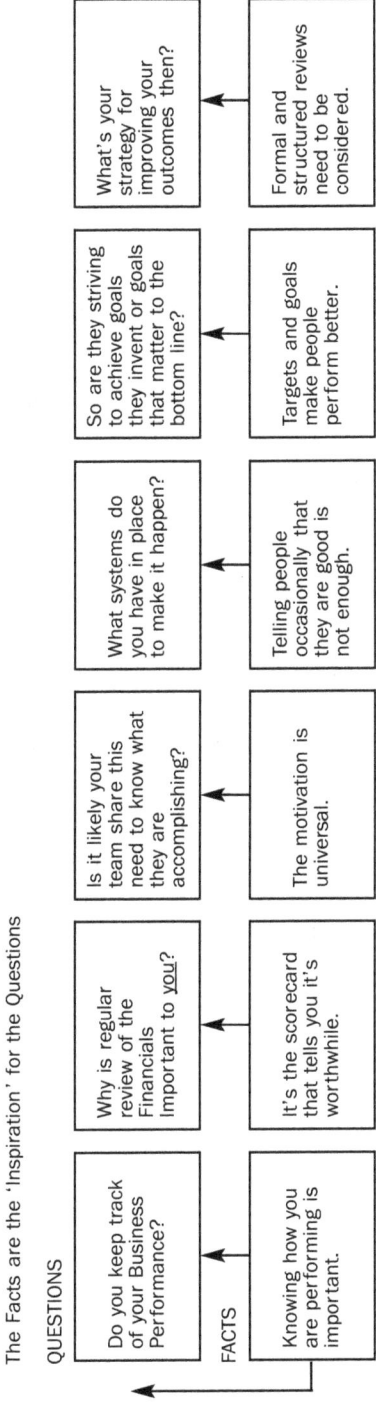

As coaches we use this Thinknig System to get clients to tell us that they need to lift their Performance Review disciplines. Note this is a Simple Thinking System because the conclusion is identified in advance.

Figure 8: Importance of Appraisal Thinking System

saying – 'If it doesn't get measured, it doesn't get done'. I would turn that upside down and say, 'If it gets measured regularly it *will* get done'.

Not measuring it doesn't necessarily mean it doesn't get done, but measuring it can guarantee it does get done. I've come to realise this, having coached or done hundreds of job descriptions in hundreds of businesses; you discover certain human limitation factors. Generally speaking an individual can be responsible for between fifty and sixty core tasks. And that will always boil down to about five or so Key Performance Indicators, five deliverables that can only happen if those fifty or sixty things are done well.

A person has to understand the five or so things on which they are going to be measured. They have to understand the way they are going to be measured and the frequency of measurement. There has to be some formality around the reporting against those measurements, and that's the way to get the best out of individuals, to get them to produce to their potential.

Imagine each staff member is in a vehicle, and they have a dashboard in front of them to tell them exactly how they're performing. In front of each staff member will be the 5 'KPI dials' so that they can track and monitor their performance every single day. People's performance/KPI's will change, particularly in growing organisations, but that's not an excuse not to do it. Reporting must be structured around the Key Performance Indicators, because KPIs then become an agenda for management and team meetings. Each person is here for those five things and that brings with it focus and clarity that move a business in the right direction.

As the workgroup leader you need to imagine all of the individual dials on your desk for everyone you supervise or employ, sort of like an airplane cockpit.

Be warned that if you stop measuring, people will notice and they will not perform as well as they would have, had they continued to be measured.

It may sound long-winded and time consuming but once these things are set up the advantages go way beyond a successful, happy, productive workgroup. The time savings are immense too. If I know what your five KPIs are, I can have a very brief but important discussion with you. It doesn't necessarily involve the weather or what you did on the weekend. I can come up to you and say how's the marketing plan – what's the inquiry level like? And when you ask questions of staff in that context it continues to reinforce how their contribution is measured, and it also makes them continually aware of the correlation between their performance and the company's performance.

One of the key characteristics of an effective workgroup is that everybody knows the score. And if everybody in the business knows the score based on a set of KPI's, this allows the business *owner* to know the score, and the business owner can then make whatever contribution *they* need to make to those KPIs, they can 'tweak' the dials. If you're letting people know on a regular basis how they're going on the five things that matter, then you've got the basis for moving them past the historical contribution of 60% of their potential.

Imagine how easy your job would become if as the workgroup leader, you could sit at your desk with your feet up with a mirror image of everybody's dashboard in front of you. Each dial would have a needle set at where productivity should be with a floating needle telling you where it actually is. If the needle falls below accepted productivity level then a buzzer lights up the dial on the desk of the staff member whose performance is not at acceptable levels. If it's not corrected within a certain period of time an electric current is sent to their chair!

Whilst this is a tongue in cheek picture, it illustrates the role of effective KPI's. Your business could in fact create such an environment – not an environment of oppression and drudgery – far from it. Your staff has a right to know the score, they have a right to feel ownership and pride for the role they play in the organisation and they have a right to appropriate and fair feedback so that they can develop and grow with the business.

Is everything measurable?

Every single thing is! People will often say, well, you can't measure everything, some important parts of an individual's job, particularly in customer service, can't be measured.

I disagree.

Everything can be benchmarked. No client has ever given a coach a key result area or Key Performance Indicator that we haven't been able to establish a measurement for.

For example, a client will say, "well we want them to treat our customers well on the phone and have a great attitude on the phone – how do you measure that?"

Very simple – you agree to survey your customers, and you set the benchmark that says, if we ring twenty customers at random, 80 per cent or more have to say that ringing us is a pleasant experience. And we're going to do that every three months – bingo!

WORKSHOP EXERCISES:

Technique 8 – My Top Five Exercise

For this exercise the workgroup member has to imagine that he or she is being transferred overseas within the company, and told that they can only reallocate 5 key responsibilities that they have. What would they be? They have to then share their selections with the group.

Note that this approach can also be used as a rudimentary way of devising what an individual's KPIs should be in the first place. It would be assumed that the workgroup member would pick the 5 most important parts of the job. This is often not the case and this process can highlight that difference of perception. The questions you need to ask, or have asked is

a) Are they really the 5 most important parts of their job?
b) If they are – how are they being measured and how can they be connected to the performance of the business?
c) If they are not – why does this person think they are?

'REALITY' CHECK

Everybody Has a Right To Know The Score is about everybody understanding the contribution they make to the outcomes for the business. Well surely if I understand that in the context of *Knowing Every Other Player's Position*, I get a better picture of the contribution I make. I also get to understand the extent to which I can impede or enhance my colleagues achieving their own outcomes.

Everybody having a right to know the score is about understanding whether both the business and you are tracking towards desired outcomes. It naturally motivates you to re-engineer your processes so you better achieve the objectives that have been set and regularly measured.

In being a natural re-inventor of your systems and procedures you're more likely to find *Hidden Duplication*. That only enhances your understanding of *Every Player's Position*, which once again makes you a better designer when it comes to designing your own pathway to success, which by now you understand you're empowered to do because the business is behaving that way.

25

BUSINESS IS A SHORTCUT TO AN OUTCOME

PRECIS:

The sixth New Reality is this: a business must be a shortcut to an outcome. The rules of accountancy may value a business by stock and other tangibles at valuation or by the increasingly shaky commodity of 'goodwill'. But the real value of a business or workgroup is how much work it saves, not how much it generates. That is: work it saves for its clients. Some businesses are actually doing their business the long way. But if a business like that doesn't find the shortest way in a hurry, its competitors will find it for them!

Once your business is a shortcut to an output, you don't even have to be unique. It's better to be unique, but even being the shortcut to something universal gives you an advantage. Or you can be unique, by producing products that are themselves shortcuts to outcomes for clients. Either way, you can't lose if your business is the shortcut and everyone else is the long way around to the same result.

THE BEHAVIOUR:

We know that businesses are strong and use more of their 'potential' when they build their processes from the client or end user backward, rather than the service forward. They also tend not to take themselves too seriously. Most importantly they take pride in their bottom line at least as much as in their work. They build their strategy from an understanding of their clients business that is often as acute as that of their own. They often have or hire expertise relevant to their clients. They develop partnerships with Clients and are always talking to them – by phone, face to face, you name it. They may even be invited to participate in brainstorming sessions with them. They are always looking for easier and faster ways to get the job done.

THE RATIONALE:

Business is a Shortcut to an Outcome means recognising that at the end of the day, people use a product or service, because it's quicker than making or doing it themselves.

For all the professionals who might be reading this book, the sobering reality is that the only reason that your clients use you is because it's quicker than getting the qualifications themselves. It's reasonable to conclude that if you could get a legal qualification out of a Cornflakes pack – although some might joke, that's where some of them come from – most people would opt for that rather than retain a lawyer. It's no different from buying a loaf of bread. The reason that people don't bake their own bread is, it is quicker to buy a loaf from the baker and, if through some miracle, it was quicker to bake it than buy it, then they would.

When a brand is a unique invention it may have some special advantage attached to it. If you totally pioneered something, people would buy only your product or service. But that's seldom the case. Commercial monogamy doesn't last long!

This new reality does not, however, mean that you should find shortcuts at the expense of the quality of your product or service. On the contrary, what it means is that once you have established and attained quality benchmarks in your business, you need to be dedicated to making it faster, to improving the process, simplifying the methodology and delivering your shortcut in the quickest possible way – without lowering those quality benchmarks.

Obviously, if there are two services offered by competing businesses, and the service quality and the price are close, the client will ultimately prefer to deal with whichever organization can deliver fastest.

One of the characteristics that were evident in effective workgroups was this constant attention and desire to speed up. It was almost like a game to see how things could be tweaked to make the product or service even better using speed as the measure rather than a 'new enhancement' or two. We have all heard the quip about complaints being a gift but in these businesses a complaint really was seen as a gift because it gave them a chance to improve.

In fact, the quality standards boom has been a major contributor to this reality. Unfortunately a system that was invented to raise the quality standards within an industry or profession has in fact meant that benchmarks for quality have been frozen. So everybody goes through a quality accreditation process to bring his or her own systems and procedures up to a particular standard, and then simply focus on maintaining that standard. A process can meet ISO standards and yet be both second best and outdated because the imposition of quality standards has resulted in stagnation of innovation. This in turn has given people a license to be complacent.

Business is a Shortcut to an Outcome is also an insight into the challenges we face in the battle with technology. The whole Technology thing is after all about just one thing. Speed. Once you can automate a process, that process naturally improves in terms of speed of delivery. Therefore it is a fruitful inclination to be looking for ways to shorten the process by automation.

Of course there is a happy medium. You get this internal competitive pressure that says, let's make sure that we meet quality standards but let's not erode our margin by exceeding those quality standards. The only basis for exceeding the quality standards is if you can increase your margin as a result of that improved quality.

Businesses can make the mistake of assuming that the quality standards they pick are the quality standards that their clients want. Then when they try to sell or impose that standard they can discover they're not going to be paid for it.

I saw a classic example of that. One of my clients was in the Printing Industry, he had invented a 'Lighting Booth'. The clever thing about this contraption was that if you put a brochure or any sort of colour object underneath its lights, it didn't matter what time of day or what climate, or what part of the hemisphere you were in, what you saw was the true appearance. (Thus if you were in Brisbane comparing your print quality against a benchmark produced, say, in Germany, using this lighting booth, you could truly compare the two.)

It was an expensive piece of equipment. As he pointed to a row of these beautiful cabinets he proclaimed, 'well we can't sell them'. The reason they were not selling however was not because of the price – it was because the industry standard itself was 'if it's as close as the naked eye will detect – it's good enough'. He once lamented . . . 'It's not like back in Europe, Aussie printers are happy with two busted fluoros in the ceiling!'

There is a point beyond which customers will not pay for excellence and as a business owner you have to know that point. It's like the staff member who delays something because they are trying to deliver to a quality standard that *they* are imposing. The output can become totally uncommercial.

It's the most frustrating experience, when somebody goes well beyond the brief you gave and then can't understand why you're totally and utterly unimpressed. Because they've taken it to an uncommercial level and in many cases they've delivered it well beyond its use-by date. Good and on time is much better than perfect and too late! Look at poor Augustin Le Prince – if he hadn't been so caught up in perfection, he might have lived longer and he, not Edison would now be known as the father of the motion picture camera!

You may be thinking to yourself at this point 'Yeah John, that may be right but what about competitive advantage through improved customer service and relationships – after all people do business with people they like'.

This is true. There is absolutely no question about that. But, even the most likable person on the planet will eventually lose the business if they can't deliver on-time, or if they fall behind their competitors in any measurable way.

Shortcuts improve relationships because the shorter the cut the more time you have to *invest* in the relationship.

If I priced the job and it takes me a certain amount of time to do the job and there's a margin in it, then I've got some time to spend building the relationship with the client. You can't build a relationship with anyone if you are consistently delivering things late or you are squeezed on margin.

When we did home renovations some years back we had a number of suppliers and tradesmen involved. The guy who bid to make the kitchen came in, listened to what we wanted. He qualified our expectations – in other words talked us out of some of the things that we were expecting, quite possibly because he was talking us into what he'd already got and already knew he could deliver perfectly. He set a date for delivery and delivered on that date. When he delivered on the date, the cabinets didn't fit; the cavity was twelve inches short. The mistake was clearly the builder's mistake, not the kitchen manufacturer's mistake. There was absolutely no discussion. He came out, assessed the situation, took one of the cabinets away and came back with a solution within three days and it was over and finished. He talked to his margin, still had some room to move and delivered a quality product while fixing someone else's mistake!

The kitchen was installed. Some of the whiz-bang things that we had had in mind weren't there, but we were totally satisfied because everything matched the expectations set by the provider, and that's a precious experience in business.

And we remember it.

The fact is most people are not hung up on perfection and an increasing level of quality – they want what was promised. And they want consistency. Just look at McDonalds – its not a 5-star gourmet experience but you could order a Big Mac in Vladivostock, Prague, Delhi or Sydney and they would all taste the same and look the same.

If you can give your customers a shortcut to what they want, when they want it, as quickly as they want it, then even if they could do it themselves – chances are they never will. (And if you can give them exactly what you promise, then you'll have them as clients next time too.)

And of course this premise works from the other perspective too. The better I understand what my clients are trying to do the better I can source the outcome. Interrogating clients about their intention is a way to find them shortcuts.

It's about finding faster ways to do what you do.

It's better matching what you do to your clients' expectations.

It's finding ways to have the client pay you less – and you doing less while still delivering the clients outcomes.

It's is about reverse engineering your clients' outcomes and applying to them the same Thinking Systems that work on your team.

WORKSHOP EXERCISES:

Technique 9

Each workgroup member must identify the 5 tasks that they are responsible for that take the longest time to complete. Imagine that a law has been passed and you now have to reduce the time it takes to complete this task.

What sacrifices would you make to do achieve the reductions?

Once each member has done this then the outcomes are to be shared with the group for discussion. With objectivity added and lessons of all the previous workshops utilised, it may be that new, faster ways are discovered.

Technique 10

Conduct a brainstorming session around the question:

How can we save our top five clients money?

'REALITY' CHECK

A Business being a Shortcut to an Outcome requires people to be motivated to make their job less, not more.

Once they understand the score, and they know how they're going to be measured, they no longer feel compelled to fill their day.

Instead, they make more intelligent choices about what they should be focusing on. Once they make more intelligent decisions about what they should be focused on, they're more inclined to be more inventive about how to improve it for themselves and their clients because we've allowed them to be the designers of their own outcomes.

Plus the quality of the design improves because they know every other player's position, and in the process the chances to uncover hidden duplication improve.

These lead to an environment where in time things don't become wrong because they never have a chance to – they're changed well before they become wrong.

26

ONLY DO WHAT ONLY YOU SHOULD DO

PRECIS:

Seventh, and the last: The secret to making people brilliant is to keep them focused on what they do brilliantly. In other words, why try to train them into being something they are not. This is where I believe your old-fashioned spruker-type motivation missed the point: it convinces people that 'anything is possible if you just believe'. I don't agree with the idea that anyone can do anything. I can't be anything, except in my dreams. But I can be brilliant at the few things I'm brilliant at!

However there is one even more fundamental principle. There is only one job that no-one in the workgroup can do, but the leader. And that job is to lead. In most businesses the leader is identifiable by the fact that they sign off leave applications, maybe hire and fire people, occasionally tell people what to do. The rest of the time is spent bending or breaking the rules in this book! For a workgroup to work, someone has to accept responsibility for getting the entity we call the team, to work as one. And there is nothing commercial about that – it is all biology.

THE BEHAVIOUR:

This is easy to spot. The leader knows the names of their staff members. They know what is important to them. A quick observation of them in the 'field' sees them acknowledge something special from a team member or ask someone's advice on an issue. They say good morning and hear it boomerang back. More than anything, you can feel it in the air when you walk into the business. They know when to celebrate. They guage the mood and do things to adjust it. They listen listen listen then talk. They have a serious mood of their own that says 'do it – don't negotiate' and they get away with it because they so often listen listen listen. People stay and have loyalty to the workgroup and the leader. They don't need legislation to make them take interest in their teams health and safety.

THE RATIONALE:

Only Do What Only You Should Do is specifically relevant to leadership of the workgroup. It means that in a workgroup of twelve people, there can only be one leader. So if it is you – be the leader.

Leadership behaviour is what paves the way for all the rest of the things we have discussed in this book to happen. Then and only then do you create an environment where the team will want to relieve you of any obligations they feel they can handle themselves.

And guess what. Inside the great Leaders, are even greater Coaches. That's what makes this material so important. Coaching is behaviour. The Four Limitations, the Seven Realities. They are simple behaviours, I know because I have seen them transform people and teams over and over again.

It doesn't mean if anyone else in the company can do the job, you shouldn't be doing it. That depends on the size of the business and the nature of the task, it may or may not be relevant. You could have procedures and systems in the business that put the business owner in a position where they're doing something *everybody* could do.

For example, phoning key intermediaries to share with them some important piece of information. That's something anyone in the company can do, but it's something the leader *should* do. *Only Do What Only You Should Do* is not about the task, it refers to the overall understanding that the one job that only you the leader can do is running the workgroup. Don't have others do it, be in control. Choose the things to do that others *could* do but you believe you *should* do – leadership.

This Reality requires you to always be occupied with the

thinking and productivity of the people in the workgroup. It's your job to understand them, it's your job to understand their strengths, adapt to their weaknesses and position people within the workgroup to allow for those differences so that you can manage the workgroup in your chosen direction.

This does not mean that being the boss is about delegating everything to everyone else while you sit at the desk with your feet up. There are plenty of people that can delegate well, but the fact that you're good at leaving things to other people doesn't make you are a good delegator. It makes you a good side-stepper but it doesn't make you a good delegator. And it doesn't make you a good boss.

DELEGATION AND LEADERSHIP

If one of the keys to being a good leader is to delegate, consider how the New Realities, through their application, position you to be the 'perfect' delegator. The reason is simple; the emergent environment provides the necessary ingredients for effective delegation. These are the three ingredients:

◆ You must suspect that the task will be done *'roughly' your way*,
◆ You must have confidence that the person you are delegating to can *actually do the task* and
◆ You must have systems in place that will *tell* you if it is not done or not done well.

But remember the critical rule of delegation: *the second best way designed by the group beats the best way imposed by the boss!*

If your business were set up to support those three things, you would become a very good delegator. You don't have to change your personality to become one, you simply allow that behaviour to emerge following the above framework. If everybody is designing their own success, and you the leader are having an opportunity to participate in that design, and if they're then telling you, the leader, how they are actually going to accomplish it, you *will* get some confidence in their ability. If they can explain to you how they're going to do it, they can do it, and as their 'coach' you will ensure that every benchmark

185

they set has some kind of measurement against it. So your delegatory powers improve. This is a classic Virtuous Circle.

Only Do What Only You Should Do is one of the realities which is specifically relevant to leadership of the workgroup yet is still important at all levels within the workgroup. At a workgroup leader's level it is to manage the workgroup. At a participant's level it is to understand the part of the job that is uniquely yours, understand where you fit in and do your bit properly. It's the most important principle, which incidentally loses its relevance somewhat as you move down through the workgroup.

Imagine a Caterpillar-grader operator sitting in his heavy machinery in that horribly uncomfortable plastic chair with eighteen levers in front of him. Your workgroup is like that and *Only Do What Only You Should Do* is about getting everybody else's hands *off* the levers. Each one of those levers represents a staff member and your job as the workgroup leader is to make sure that no one touches anyone else's lever.

BUSINESS OWNER 'CONUNDRUMS'

There are some unbelievable conundrums in business and my own story illustrates one of them. I invented a way to help businesses improve. It was my hobby. And I started to run – my apologies for using the word – a consultancy, where I promoted my methodology and I started to make a really good living. I was working with my clients and proving my methodology and was learning about the way we process information, the way we think and it was just heaven.

And I worked out that there were some parts of the job that I didn't enjoy doing, like developing the marketing collateral and the technology platform and producing the output from the workshops and so on. Naturally the thought occurred to me that if somebody else did those jobs for me, then life would be perfect. So I then decided to build a company that actually answered that challenge, providing Coaches with an environment where they only did the things they loved while someone looked after the 'grind'. And now what do I do? I run a team responsible for the grind! I never get to the stuff that made me want to start this thing in the first place! So I wrote a book instead!

The conundrum is: when people are good at something and

decide to go into business for themselves, the minute they do, they are on their way to not doing what they are good at anymore. The moment you go into business for yourself and start to hire staff you are in the people management business and that's the big business you are in. And few people realize that.

If somebody actually gave you a pill that allowed you to experience all of the highs and lows of marriage, you might never get married. What keeps you married is that the good and bad are separated, so you have moments of joy and moments of challenge. And when you have a moment of challenge, you look forward to a moment of joy. But if you knew what you were getting yourself into, in many cases you wouldn't do it. So it is in a business – if there was a pill that allowed people to experience what being in business is like, I believe 70 per cent of people who do go into business wouldn't even start. Because what it is and what they think it is are two different things.

So why is it so hard? People are bad at managing people because they've never been taught to. People are bad at managing people because the process of managing people is complicated. People think it is an enormous challenge. Hopefully, by the time you have read this book you'll understand the things you need to know about managing thinking, and if you can manage the thinking you can manage the people. It's not hard to do. It's hard to understand, but it is not hard to do. Follow the excersises. Behave like a leader and people will think you are one, and then you are one!

The New Realities are not pills that you can swallow to make your business better. They are strategies for leadership behaviour that you can easily replicate, resulting in better outcomes and ultimately better business.

KEYS TO EFFECTIVE LEADERSHIP

We have found that there are a number of characteristics that leaders display.

ACCEPTING THE ROLE

Being the leader of your business is your *first* and *primary* responsibility. What you do for a living, that is what product or service your company delivers, comes second (to you). Service and product are the number one responsibility for the team, the team is the number one responsibility for you!

That does not mean that your team takes more of your time but it does take more of your focus. Unless by some fluke you happen to have high level Human Resource Management skills, you are by definition battling with a lesser skill. A few people do have these skills, but invariably they are inherent. They can of course be learnt but that takes time and focus.

I spend more time in front of audiences talking about business coaching than I do face to face with my staff. But the former is something I'm 'good' at – well if I'm not I bloody well should be after the time that I've spent doing it! This activity for me takes a lot of time but not a lot of 'focus'.

On the other hand, when it's appraisal time at work it takes less time but a lot more focus. See, even as a business coach it is still not something that I do often enough for it to be automatic.

Look at your diary and think about your 'Leadership Time', review your meeting schedule. Think of each staff member and ask the question. 'When is my regular time for getting to know each one?' 'When is my regular time for formally letting them know how they are going?' 'When is my regular time for introducing them to some other aspect of what we do?' 'When is their regular time for finding out how the business is going etc?'

Leadership in this context is not about leading teams, it is about understanding and knowing people, individuals, and developing them into a team with their co-operation.

This, in turn, is not about psychology it is about behaviour. It can't be about psychology because most of the good leaders I know are not psychologists! Their behaviours, not their knowledge are what draw the team around them. When you start to get to know your people and they see you taking a direct interest in them, they will draw the conclusion that you are the leader. We can write a psychology textbook on why this level of communication is important to people. Fortunately someone else has written the book, and even more fortunately we don't have to read it to be good leaders!

Rule number one is to accept the job and be seen to do so.

Cautionary Note: If you feel you have been neglecting this

responsibility please don't announce to the team – 'I've decided to take the leadership role seriously, I feel I've let you all down and have not taken enough interest in you as individuals or as a team . . . so I am going to dedicate myself to accepting responsibility as a leader of this team.' This actually translates to 'The boss has been to another bloody seminar . . . s/he'll get over it!'

A word about Talent and Natural Ability

Think about this . . .

Suppose I was to hook up with Pat Rafter – I hear he's a personable guy – and ask him if I can follow him around for three years. And in those three years I do exactly what he does. I eat when he eats and I eat what he eats. I play and practice when he plays and practices. I sleep when he sleeps. It won't matter because at the end of those three years I just won't be no Pat Rafter! I will be a better tennis player because I have learnt and improved my skill but I will not be a champion because tennis is neither my natural ability nor my talent, it's not what I'm built for.

This whole premise that we can do anything we put our mind to is, in my view the greatest lie perpetrated against humanity by the so-called motivational industry.

It's simply not true!

Talent is natural ability combined with a desire to repeat. For example Karen has natural ability as a writer but she only became brilliant because of her desire to repeat – to keep writing, both were natural abilities. Combined, they are the makings of a talent. By doing so her natural writing ability is combined with the increased level of skill, which moves her closer toward excellence. (By the way Karen wrote this!)

The talented sports person you knew at school, who 'never amounted to much because they didn't apply themselves' was not in fact talented at all. They had Natural Ability, which without the desire to repeat, is all it ever will be.

So whilst there are certain things you can be if you put your mind to it – excellence in those areas is only possible by also having the natural gift and supplementing that gift with learnt skill and repetition.

UNDERSTAND THE THINGS LEADERS DO

There are many things leaders do. Let's focus on the five most important.

1. They care about their people

Caring about your people does not mean become everyone's best friend or the company confidante. We all know that there is a fine line when it comes to staff/employer relationships. Many unfortunately err on the side of conservatism. You can be aloof and still lead, although that is a rare skill. Simply put, if the staff believe that you have even a passing interest in their life outside work, they are more likely to want to help you achieve your goals when it comes to the business itself.

This can be as simple as remembering their name! For extra brownie points remember the names of their spouses and kids and the milestones they face (weddings, birthdays, etc). It also helps when discussing these things to mention what was said last time and listen and remember what is said for next time. Please don't read this as becoming the social conscience for your firm! Leave that to the party animals but do make a personal connection at some level.

Do people do the job because you pay them, or because they want to do their bit AND you pay them? Remember getting paid is WHY people work, enjoyment in the team and ownership of the job is HOW they work.

2. They let facts arrive before emotions

How many times have you let your emotions affect an issue for what eventually turns out to be no good reason? Understand that if someone is enjoying an emotional moment, they are going to give you the 'facts' in a way that has the highest chance of leading you to the same emotional moment – so you can 'share'! Effective leaders don't play this game.

They will identify quickly the things they need to know, before they should draw a conclusion based on those facts. If they can't get the facts straight away, they keep their emotions on hold until the facts arrive. This does not mean that they are NOT emotional. Quite the contrary because when you have all the facts and a particular conclusion is evident; you have confidence matched with the emotions, which is a powerful combination indeed.

3. They avoid being roadblocks

Leaders know when their team is relying on them for a contribution to a task so that they can continue with their job. Think of the message it sends if *you* hold up the project.

Whether you like it or not it gives a very clear message about the importance not only of the job, but also of the person doing the job. Being quick to respond or deliver sets off a positive sequence of events through the business like a row of dominos collapsing through the business. If you respond slowly, your staff has the right to continue forward slowly. In this sense the leader is the pacesetter.

'Do what I say not as I do' is a cliché created from this premise. However at the end of the day 'Actions speak louder than words!'

Task for each morning: write down in your diary the names of the people that are waiting for you. Don't write the task only, be sure to connect to the actual person that is waiting for you to complete something so that they can earn their living . . .

4. They talk in Key Performance Indicators (KPIs)

Leaders have relevant and meaningful business discussions with their staff. Through this they also ensure that people know how they make an individual contribution to the business outcomes and help their staff turn their key tasks into Key Performance Indicators (KPIs). As we mentioned earlier, people are not necessarily interested in the performance of the company unless and until they can see a direct correlation between that performance and what they do as individuals each day. Every staff member has a right to know how he or she influences the business outcomes. Once made known, the interaction between leaders and staff can touch on topics of personal interest, followed by a series of focussed questions on KPIs. It sends a heap of powerful messages about the level of awareness the leader has. Remember if people think you are watching they behave as if you are!

5. They invite invention

It's more important to have it done to 'your standard' than it is to have it you're 'your way'. The difference is subtle but very powerful and leaders know it, often unconsciously. If you focus on the outcomes and work backward you discover that there are many ways to get there.

However the best way not embraced with passion is not as

good as the second best way delivered with team commitment. Everything about a team members' contribution to the business improves when they are allowed to *suspect* that they are in control.

FINAL THOUGHTS

If you are an accomplished leader then I hope these few observations have helped re-enforce your already powerful behaviour. On the other hand if, like me, you are still developing those skills I hope these observations help you on your journey.

Remember, take charge, it's the one job that sets you apart from the rest.

Dedicate time to the challenge, reach out to members of your team: you don't coach teams, you coach individuals into teams. Let them know what's important and keep reminding them, set the pace for the business, and let the team have a stake in their job, if not the company. Oh and be cool, better decisions are made when facts are collected first and emotions follow!

WORKSHOP EXERCISE

Technique 11

As the workgroup leader, list all the things that you have done in the last five days that are exclusively motivated by your responsibility to lead.

Now think about how you intend to advance on the situation.

List the names of your staff. Then next to each the name of their 'significant other'. List their hobby or pastimes.

'REALITY' CHECK

When you've got a team working with the previous six New Realities, finally you have a platform to allow the business owner to *Only Do What You Should Do.*

You can't lead a team unless they invite you to. The extent to which they would invite you is largely driven by the degree of *'invention'* you allow them.

Until you are free to take the helicopter view, helpful deliberate *shortcuts* and *duplication* will likely endure. This helps you identify those things that remain for *you* to do, and allows you to step up, take the job and lead the people.

The only way to lead in a commercial context is to be sure that your teams *know the score.*

27

THE NEW REALITIES AS VIRTUOUS CIRCLES

We repeat the Reality Checks here to allow the Virtuous Circle to be closed . . .

Design equals motivation means people perform better when they're given an opportunity to design their own success. *Know Every Other Players Position* is about understanding what everybody else in the company does. Understanding what everybody else in the company does makes you a better designer, so by helping people understand what everyone in the company does, and then empowering them to design their own solutions, you now have somebody who's likely to design solutions that are closer to the leading edge. This is why you've got this virtuous improvement all the time in business. I design a way to do something, I find out more about what you do, I get a chance to re-design, and each time I increase my potential. Remember that a journey towards potential will always improve it.

Hidden duplication is about making sure that you're not doing two different things in order to achieve the same outcome. Surely my chances of finding hidden duplication rely on my opportunity to understand every other player's position. If I know what the other people in the company do, I'm more likely to find hidden duplication, and if I find that hidden duplication and you empower me to be the designer of my own solution, then I will re-design it to improve it and avoid hidden duplication.

In time right becomes wrong means that eventually the processes and systems in the business will become out of date.

Well surely, if I understand every other player's position, I'm more motivated to identify where the potential weaknesses in the process are. If I'm allowed to and encouraged to be the designer of my own methodology or my own process, I'm more likely to be looking for those parts of my job or those parts of my processes and procedures that are likely to become redundant. I'm more likely to look at them because (a) you gave me the opportunity and (b) because I now see it as my responsibility. I'm empowered – I know that I'm allowed to, and therefore I'm more inclined to. In many cases people don't re-engineer because they don't think that it's their role or that they've got the authority to re-engineer.

Everybody has a right to know the score is about everybody understanding the contribution they make to the outcome for the business. Well surely if I understand that in the context of knowing every other player's position, I get a better picture of the contribution I make. Not only that I get to understand the extent to which I can impede or enhance my colleagues achieving their own outcomes. Everybody having a right to know the score is about understanding whether the business and whether you are tracking towards your outcomes. It naturally motivates you to re-engineer your processes and procedure so you better achieve the objectives that have been set. In being a natural re-inventor of your systems and procedures you're more likely to find hidden duplication and that only enhances your understanding of every player's position. That, once again, makes you a better designer when it comes to designing your own pathway to success, which by now you understand you're empowered to do because the business is behaving that way.

A business being a shortcut to an outcome requires people to be motivated to make their job less, not more. Once they understand the score, and they know how they're going to be measured, they no longer feel compelled to fill their day. Instead, they make more intelligent choices about what they should be focusing on. Once they make more intelligent decisions about what they should be focused on, they're more inclined to be more inventive about how to improve it for themselves and their clients, because we've allowed them to be the designers of their own outcomes. Plus the quality of the design improves because they know every other player's position, and in the process the chances of hidden duplication being uncovered improve. These then lead to a natural environment where in time things don't become wrong because they never have a chance to – they're changed well before they become wrong.

And when you've got a team working like that, finally you have a platform to allow the business owner to *Only do what the business owner should do*. It helps you identify those things that remain for you to do, and allows you to step up, take the job and lead the people.

28

ENGINEERING VIRTUOUS CIRCLES, OVERCOMING THE FOUR LIMITATIONS

We've looked at the realities of business, the challenges we face and finally the New Realities. So why does implementing these New Realities into your business make such a radical difference? How do they mitigate the Four Limitations?

If I let you be the designer of your own process, that forces me to articulate exactly what my expectations are, and allows you to articulate exactly what you perceive them to be. What's happened? Communication has improved. We've forced ourselves to use the same benchmarks or the same definitions for each of the bits of language. We have avoided the challenge to our thinking process brought on by the fact that language has no consistently, universally understood dictionary.

First, when you sit down and say to somebody, tell me what you want to accomplish, and they identify that, and then you force them to describe exactly how they're going to accomplish it. You're starting to raise your 'picture paints (that is needs) a thousand words' ratio from 70 to possibly 300–400. And it has not taken you any extra energy, because it's the person 'doing the doing' who's going to articulate how they anticipate doing it.

The second thing is that if I'm the business owner and I don't have to do the job, I have some objectivity about how it ought to be done. I'm also subjective because when the business started I might have done it a certain way. Let's look at that a different way. I'm the business owner, and you're the employee.

There is a process that I want done, and I have a certain point of view about it. You have some experience with it that's why you were hired.

What we now have is a mixture of subjectivity and objectivity in each of our minds. I'm subjective because I have a way that I want it done, but I'm objective because I have the business' overriding responsibilities and profitability to deliver. So I have to be prepared to negotiate to some extent. You on the other hand have an objective point of view about the way my company does it because you weren't there when it was invented. That's matched against your subjective skills, knowledge and experience. By bringing those two points of view together in a constructive environment, we do have a chance of negotiating a best way to do something.

So what the New Realities actually do is allow us to circumvent each and every shortcoming of thinking that stops or at least holds us back from our true potential.

I can remember going to see a client of mine who indicated that his company was about to go through an acquisition. He was excited and very animated about this new stage of his business. Not wanting to burst his bubble but also having an obligation to him as a client and friend, I asked if they had done their due diligence. Due diligence is nothing more than the process of checking to see that the business is what you think the business is.

My client, looking rather shocked at the question, told me that they had done due diligence, and whilst he appreciated the question the fact was the business he was buying belonged to a friend and colleague. My client, it turned out had known the seller for a long time and known the business, so apparently already had a fair degree of understanding about that company, and a reasonable relationship with the owner.

My next question was, 'Tell me, just out of interest, does that make the due diligence *more* important, or *less* important?'

I will never forget the look on his face when I asked that question, you could almost hear the cogs turning in his mind and he stopped dead in his tracks. I silently watched as the expression on his face changed as he realised the inescapable conclusion that precisely because of that friendship and that history, the due diligence became not just vital, but imperative.

The really, really scary part was that it was at that exact same moment that I realised that six months prior to this meeting I had made the exact same fatal error of treating an acquisition in exactly the same way as my client. My company had acquired a business and our due diligence had been less than ruthless because we knew and trusted the business owner. I remember to this day the moment I realised my mistake – I felt physically sick at what I had done. It was the biggest, most expensive and most painful business mistake I have ever made. If you get nothing else from this book please gets this: The right question is *everything*. I could have avoided my mistake, I should have avoided it but I hadn't asked the right questions.

My client was luckier, he had a coach, and prompted by the above dialogue, they went into extensive, impartial and thorough due diligence. And strangely enough, once the due diligence process started the 'friend' who was the seller, elected not to sell the company to that particular buyer but sold it to somebody else who was left to later discover some of the hidden challenges in that company.

The right question saved a fortune. The right question saved agony. The right question avoided unnecessary energy being wasted.

One question can make or break a business. One question can make or break a relationship. One question can make or break an experiment. One question, at the right time, is everything. The danger we face is presuming that finding that question is some sort of liquid piece of creativity – that if we have the right experience in the right background at the right moment, the right question will indeed emerge.

That's a crock of bull, I mean, everybody reading this book has had that wonderful experience where six months – six weeks – six hours or six minutes after the event, you think of what you should have said! The point is, my friends, if we think about the outcomes that we hope to accomplish and they are all predictable, and they can all be determined before the endeavour begins, then we can distil a right set of questions to ask before we even start the journey.

Business is tough, it's bloody near impossible, precisely

because – in my view – businesses are actually built to fail, not succeed. You read earlier that people come to a business from many different backgrounds. Just the nature of the personality and background of the people you need to make a business effective is a recipe for poor communication.

If you get two accountants talking about something that is of a financial nature, you have a better chance of them understanding each other than if the Marketing Director talks to the Production Manager about something financial. In the latter case the two of them may be using words they don't understand to discuss a language they've never learnt, to convey principles that they are totally ignorant about.

So in that environment where you've got the Production Manager, the Marketing Manager, the Operations Manager, the business owner and the Sales Manager all talking, you have a recipe for communication failure. It shouldn't surprise people that businesses fail. It should surprise people that businesses succeed!

When we as businesspersons go into business, we typically reach for a service to guide us through the above challenges. Sadly, historically, providing that service has fallen to a profession totally incapable of fulfilling those expectations for themselves, let alone for their clients. You all know the profession about which I'm speaking – Accountants.

Have you every stopped to think that accountants must have seen every conceivable mistake that businesses had or could or will ever make. Yet their clients keep making them!

And that has been a major motivator for writing this book – helping people understand that there really is no excuse for repeating errors, there's no reason for making mistakes that others have already made, and there is a formula for avoiding those pitfalls. There is a natural and obvious set of questions that needs to be attached to every decision that anyone ever makes, and those questions are the Thinking Systems. What we've been able to identify, working with thousands of workgroups at BTS is that there is one best set of questions to apply to every situation or challenge. You can significantly reduce or eliminate errors in business and significantly impr ove the quality of business performance by the application of these Thinking Systems.

Accountants get paid even when people make mistakes, so there's a significant motivation for them to watch the accident happen. Business coaches give you the map to help navigate through the intersection. Accountants are the tow trucks waiting at dangerous intersections for those without a map!

There will be a future, I promise you, when people will decide to go into business and the first ally they will search for will not be an accountant – it will be a business coach. Join the ranks of the smart business thinkers and get yourself a coach!

Good luck.

'Life in business is a long journey, not an overnighter, so pack carefully . . .'

~ John Vamos

ACKNOWLEDGEMENTS

For the Source Code to the Thinking System and the keys to my potential: my parents Kathy and Peter Vamos, and brothers Steve and Mike.

For their willingness to test the idea before I even understood it: Martin Pisani, Michael Murray and Barry Moore.

For showing me how to explain what I meant and giving me a language that could connect my thinking to the rest of the planet: Bruce Haddon.

For taking my ideas and showing me how they needed to 'sound' to make a good story: Karen Macreadie.

For unwavering support for the 'cause': Ross Teakle, Sally North, Anesan Naidoo, Jennifer Zeitch, Janette Thorogood, Susan Flack and Harry Fox.

For their support and confidence in BTS: Rob Dillon, Denis Fitzgerald, Ian Elliot, Bill Grant, Mark Bramston, Terry Youngman, Steve Cameron, Terry Lawler, Clare Loewenthal, Stefan Ackerie, Brian Sher, Bill Radcliffe, Bill Loewenthal, Gavin Partridge, Russell Stanfield, Wayne Bubb, Alan Wickes.

THIS BOOK IS DEDICATED: To my wife and best friend Yvette Vamos

To Mum, Dad, Lesley, Alex, Lily-Anne and Pauline.

To all the clients of BTS and the 30,000 plus people that have been the subject of our processes. Their contribution made the conclusions in this book possible.

To the BTS Coaches who showed respect for the knowledge that Thinking Systems unlock in all of us.

To the memory of Terry Driscoll, the 'QAM'.

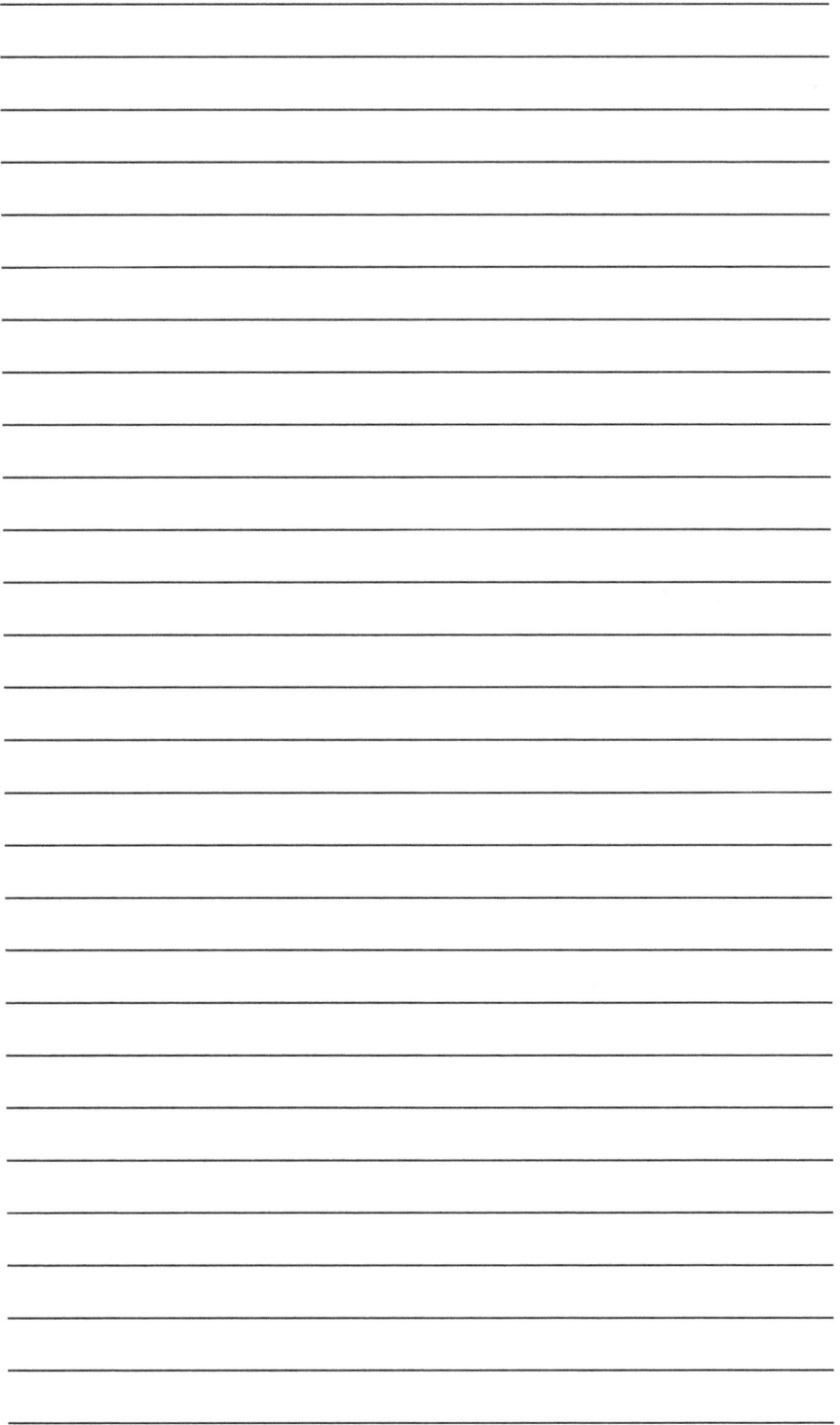

www.ingramcontent.com/pod-product-compliance
Lightning Source LLC
Chambersburg PA
CBHW070658190326
41458CB00053B/6926/J